All the Roads Are Open

An Afghan Journey, 1939–1940

ANNEMARIE SCHWARZENBACH

TRANSLATED AND INTRODUCED BY
ISABEL FARGO COLE

WITH AN AFTERWORD BY ROGER PERRET

T0065640

LONDON NEW YORK CALCUTTA

GOETHE INSTITUT

This publication was supported by a grant from the Goethe-Institut India

swiss arts council
pr☐helvetia

The original English publication of this book was supported by a grant from
Pro Helvetia, Swiss Arts Council

Seagull Books, 2021

Annemarie Schwarzenbach, *Alle Wege sind offen*
© Lenos Verlag, Basel, 2008
First published in English translation by Seagull Books, 2011
English translation © Isabel Fargo Cole, 2011

ISBN 978 0 85742 822 6

British Library Cataloguing-in-Publication Data
A catalogue record for this book is available from the British Library

Typeset by Seagull Books, Calcutta, India
Printed by WordsWorth India, New Delhi, India

CONTENTS

How does one do justice to a woman who drove a Ford across the Hindu Kush yet died after falling from her bicycle near her Swiss home at the age of thirty-four?

Annemarie Schwarzenbach is a European cult figure: journalist, novelist, antifascist, archaeologist, morphine addict, world traveller. It is her travel writing—a significant part of her oeuvre—that best illuminates her complex, multifaceted personality. And her journey to Afghanistan with Ella Maillart from 1939 to 1940 is one of her life's most telling episodes, an ambitious, fruitful failure. Maillart's account of the journey and her troubled friendship with Schwarzenbach, *The Cruel Way* (London, 1947), stands as a classic of travel literature. Sadly, it failed to bring broader attention to Schwarzenbach's life and work, since at the insistence of her mother, Renée, she was fictionalized in the narrative as 'Christina'. To this day, Annemarie Schwarzenbach remains virtually unknown to the English-speaking world.

By insisting on the pseudonym, Renée Schwarzenbach was merely having the last word in a protracted struggle between the Schwarzenbach family and its black sheep. The second of Alfred and Renée Schwarzenbach's four children, Annemarie was born on 23 May 1908 and brought up in Bocken bei Horgen, the family's luxurious estate on Lake Zurich. The Schwarzenbachs were one of Switzerland's wealthiest industrialist families. A politically conservative scion of the Bismarck family, the charismatic, imperious Renée was the household's dominant figure. As a passionate music patron, she turned Bocken into a magnet for figures such as Richard Strauss, Wilhelm Fürtwängler and the Wagner clan. Indeed, for several decades, she maintained a discreet romance with Wagnerian soprano Emmy Krüger, a friend of the family whose relationship with Řenée seems to have been tacitly accepted by the good-natured Alfred. As a child, Renée had wished to be a boy; as a mother, she transferred this wish to her favourite daughter, Annemarie. Into Annemarie's teen years she liked to dress her daughter as a boy and spoke of her playfully as her 'page'.

Annemarie studied history in Zurich and Paris, receiving her doctorate in 1931, at the age of twenty-three. That same year, her first novel was published. But despite all her talents and privileges, only her child-hood—a frequent, yearning motif in her work—could remotely be described as carefree. She felt attracted to women early on, and with her androgynous beauty (she had 'the face of an inconsolable angel', according to Roger Martin du Gard) she was soon embroiled in scandalous affairs far less discreet than her mother's. No one was more scandalized than Renée, whose reactions seem to reflect a complex mixture of envy, possessiveness and fear of scandal. Annemarie remained dependent on her mother all her life, both financially and emotionally, and despite her frequent rebellions Renée never cut off her often manipulative support.

At the age of twenty-two, Annemarie met Klaus and Erika Mann, Thomas Mann's children, who helped emancipate her from her mother and had a profound influence on her life. The Mann siblings, both left-wing gay intellectuals, opened up a world in which she could live out her sexuality and her artistic ambitions. But they also introduced her, directly or indirectly, to morphine, an addiction that would haunt her for the rest of her life. Her lifelong relationship with the Mann siblings was often rocky due to her emotional instability, her unrequited passion for Erika Mann and political tensions with the reactionary Schwarzenbach clan.

In 1931, Annemarie moved to Berlin; her *Lyrische Novelle* (*Lyric Novella*), a story of a young 'man's' infatuation with a variété singer, reflects the decadence and the desperation of her sojourn at the end of the Weimar Republic. It appeared at a most inopportune time— March 1933, just months after Hitler's seizure of power. By then the Manns had already left Germany for good. Schwarzenbach left Berlin in April.

From October 1933 to April 1934 she travelled, often alone, through Turkey, Syria, Lebanon, Palestine, Iraq and Persia. The first of her major journeys, it launched her career as a photojournalist, with numerous articles and photo reports appearing in major Swiss newspapers. Her book about the journey, *Winter in Vorderasien* (Winter in the Middle East) appeared in 1934.

Like the Afghan journey several years later, this odyssey was in part an escape from Europe's political nightmare. By contrast, in the meantime the Mann siblings had become leading figures in Europe's literary and antifascist exile scene. Schwarzenbach supported their initiatives, such as Klaus' magazines *Die Sammlung* and, later, *Decision*. In August 1934, she travelled with Klaus to the First Soviet Writers' Congress in Moscow, on which she reported with a sympathetic yet critical eye. However, the Manns were often sceptical of her ability to contribute to the antifascist cause, and Schwarzenbach was plagued by feelings of inadequacy as she sought to take political action while hampered by her own battle with depression and addiction—and with her family. The 'Pfeffermühle scandal' ultimately caused a serious rupture.

Renée had always taken exception to Annemarie's friendship with the Manns. In November 1934, with Annemarie back in Persia on an archaeological expedition, the conflict came to a head. The Pfeffermühle, Erika Mann's legendary political cabaret in Zurich, was disrupted by a gang of pro-fascist rowdies led by Annemarie's cousin James and ultimately forced to close. The Manns suspected Renée's involvement and took Annemarie to task for it. Immediately upon her return, Annemarie took up the matter with her family and openly expressed her support for the antifascists. Her relationship with the Manns suffered nonetheless.

Under the strain, Annemarie attempted suicide in January 1935. That April, she travelled to Teheran to marry the French diplomat Claude Clarac, whom she had met the previous year in Persia. The two were deeply attached to each other, but it appears to have been largely a marriage of convenience (Clarac was also gay). For Schwarzenbach, it seemed to offer a certain respectability, stability and independence from her parents—and the diplomatic passport proved useful in her travels. But the role of a diplomatic wife with all its social obligations proved too constrictive. Ultimately a tortured love affair with the consumptive daughter of the Turkish ambassador (the inspiration for her novel *Das glückliche Tal*, The Happy Valley, 1938), a bout of malaria and renewed morphine abuse brought the experiment to a tragic end. She and Clarac remained married but went their separate ways.

In October 1936, she accepted the invitation of her friend Barbara Hamilton-Wright to travel to America, where Erika Mann was working on the American debut of the Pfeffermühle. While Schwarzenbach's renewed drug consumption put a strain on her relationship with Erika, in January 1937 she pulled herself together to travel with Hamilton-Wright through Pennsylvania, reporting on the 'dark side' of the mining and steel industry. In the summer of 1937, after a stay in Switzerland, she travelled through the Baltic countries, with a keen eye for the tense political situation, and to Moscow, where she recovered the lost documents of the famous Swiss mountaineer Lorenz Saladin, who had died in 1936 while climbing in the Tian Shan mountains. The resulting book, *Lorenz Saladin: Ein Leben für die Berge* (Lorenz Saladin: A Life for the Mountains, 1938), was Schwarzenbach's most commercially successful work. In September 1937, Schwarzenbach returned to America; this time she and Hamilton-Wright travelled in the South as photojournalists, focusing especially on social conflicts in industrial regions, the role of the trade unions and the positive effects of the New Deal.

After the German annexation of Austria in March 1938, Schwarzenbach played a more active role in the antifascist resistance. She wrote articles, most of which proved too political for publication, liaised between the German exiles and the antifascist underground in Austria and apparently used her diplomatic passport to rescue many Austrian antifascists. However, she continued to struggle with morphine addiction, which she saw as a shameful weakness. In a clinic in Yverdon, in the autumn of 1938, she recovered long enough to write what many regard as her best work: *Das glückliche Tal*, a fictionalized account of her 1935 sojourn in Persia, which appeared in September 1939. By that time Schwarzenbach was already in Kabul with writer Ella Maillart, a new adventure that she felt was a chance to take her life into her hands. In his afterword to this collection, Roger Perret describes the Afghan journey and the complex circumstances of Schwarzenbach's life at that time.

Schwarzenbach returned to Europe in February 1940 with the renewed desire to assist the German antifascist exiles. In May 1940, she returned to America, where she joined the Mann siblings in their commitment to the Emergency Rescue Committee, established to assist opponents of the Nazis. Schwarzenbach built up contacts with American newspapers and considered writing in English; she was having difficulties publishing her political work even in 'neutral' Switzerland and saw America as her only hope of finding an audience.

In the summer of 1940, the Mann siblings introduced Schwarzenbach to Carson McCullers, who fell in love with her. Schwarzenbach was unable to reciprocate the younger woman's feelings. The strain of extricating herself took its toll, especially as she was already engaged in a difficult relationship with Margot von Opel. To make matters worse, her father—with whom she had had a much more harmonious relationship than with Renée—died in November. Following a suicide attempt in a New York hotel that December, Schwarzenbach was admitted to a psychiatric clinic in Greenwich, Connecticut. After a dramatic escape, she was forcibly hospitalized in Bellevue, diagnosed with schizophrenia and subjected to several weeks of brutal treatment. In February 1941, she was released under the condition that she leave the country immediately. At about the same time, McCullers' novel *Reflections in a Golden Eye* appeared, dedicated to Schwarzenbach.

Later that spring, after a stay in Lisbon, Schwarzenbach travelled to the Belgian Congo where she worked on journalistic pieces and a novel, *Das Wunder des Baums* (The Miracle of the Tree). She increasingly came into conflict with the authorities, later claiming that they had accused her of being a German spy. The manuscript of *Das Wunder des Baums* shows signs of mental strain, and it is thought that Schwarzenbach may have been suffering from paranoia herself. In March 1942, Schwarzenbach returned to Lisbon, then travelled to Rabat, Morocco, to spend several weeks with Claude Clarac. She had hoped to discuss divorce, but they so enjoyed their time together that they agreed to maintain the marriage. Schwarzenbach went home to Switzerland, promising to join him in Morocco that autumn.

Schwarzenbach continued to correspond with McCullers, one of her letters inspiring the latter to write the story 'A Tree. A Rock. A Cloud'. The two writers planned to translate each other's work.

On 7 September, Schwarzenbach suffered head injuries in a bicycle accident—showing off for a friend, she had been riding with no hands. Though she lived for several more weeks, Renée and the doctors permitted no visitors—not even Clarac, who had travelled to Switzerland as soon as he heard of the accident. Supposedly, they wished to spare friends the sight of Annemarie, who was conscious but had succumbed entirely to 'mental illness'. The nature of this 'illness' was variously diagnosed by her baffled doctors as schizophrenia and the toxic effects of drug abuse; in consultation with Renée, they relinquished all efforts to heal Annemarie and simply kept her sedated with, ironically enough, morphine. She died on 15 November 1942 in Sils.

After Annemarie's death, in express defiance of her written will, Renée destroyed many of her letters and papers which she felt reflected badly upon the family.

Schwarzenbach's work, so little recognized in her lifetime, was rediscovered in Switzerland in the late

1980s. In a veritable explosion of interest, the bulk of her journalistic and literary work and much of her photography has since been published, mainly by Lenos Verlag in Basel. Understandably, her striking image and dramatic life has led to a certain cult of personality that often eclipses her writing itself, with some romanticizing her literary achievements while others, perhaps in reaction, downplay them. Whether Schwarzenbach achieved artistic perfection, or even her full artistic potential, is an unanswerable question. But more than adulation or (morbid) fascination, she deserves respect for the talent, moral integrity and professionalism with which she confronted, and often transcended, her own weaknesses and the turbulence of the times. In her short life, she left us an oeuvre of astounding range and richness.

A NOTE ON THE TEXT
AND TRANSLATION

The pieces in this collection (originally published as *Alle Wege sind offen*, Lenos Verlag, 2008) were selected by editor Roger Perret; some had appeared in Swiss newspapers between 1939 and 1940, while some were previously unpublished. Due to the varying sources, some slight overlaps and repetitions occur. The order of the essays more or less reflects her itinerary. As Perret describes in the Afterword, the two women set out from Geneva in June 1939 and drove through the Balkans, Turkey and Persia, arriving in Kabul in August, where they learned of the outbreak of war in Europe. In October, they parted ways. Maillart went to India; Schwarzenbach returned north to Turkistan for several weeks and then travelled to India herself, meeting Maillart in Bombay in January 1940 before boarding the ship to Europe.

Schwarzenbach is inconsistent in her renderings of place names. To quote Perret:

> As a rule, we did not standardize divergent renditions of place names such as Trapezunt/ Trabzon or Persia/Iran. This apparent inconsistency reflects not only a historically conditioned uncertainty as to the 'correct' spelling of place names on a foreign continent, but also a phenomenon characteristic of the author's writing

process: seduction by exotic, magical-sounding names.

In my translation I have retained conscious anachronisms (Stamboul, Trapezunt, Persia), but for all other place names I have chosen whatever appears to be the most common current transliteration (there are often numerous variants) to assist readers who would like to trace Schwarzenbach's route on today's map.

In some cases, I have drawn on Maillart's account for information. Comparing these two accounts of the same journey is a fascinating and often moving experience, material enough for a whole essay. I have merely noted some instances in which Schwarzenbach's account diverges in slight but illuminating ways. Perhaps most strikingly—and I mention this to prevent confusion—in a number of places Schwarzenbach speaks only of 'I' even when describing parts of the journey that she and Maillart experienced together (as in 'Therapia', 'The Steppe', 'The Prisoners'). This might seem churlish, especially in light of Maillart's account, which offers a deeply felt portrait of Schwarzenbach herself and an examination of their friendship. But Maillart wrote her book years later, in the shadow of Schwarzenbach's death, while Schwarzenbach, back in 1939, was writing for the newspapers and did not thematize her difficult but lasting friendship with Maillart. To a startling extent, these newspaper pieces vibrate with naked emotion and intimations of private turmoil—but in an encrypted, poetic manner. And they occasionally take poetic license. This switch from 'we' to 'I' is a device that reflects Schwarzenbach's permanent sense of existential isolation while lending the journey a universality and dream-like immediacy.

Isabel Fargo Cole
February 2011

Part One

MOUNT ARARAT

We'd been told about the Balkan roads, and a whole chapter could be written on them, easily, gladly, now that our Ford, all struggles put behind it, is sailing down the coast of Anatolia, stowed on the deck of the Turkish steamship *Ankara*. Our map showed an 'International Road' from Trieste via Zagreb to Belgrade, from Belgrade to Sofia, from Sofia straight to Istanbul. Certainly, this road exists: past the capital of Yugoslavia came eighty kilometres of asphalt, from Lüleburgaz to Constantinople even more than a hundred kilometres, and long stretches were under construction, which should have been some comfort. But where there was construction we no longer had a road; we drove through the open fields. In Bulgaria, we were sent down a bridle-path, through a mountain valley of fantastic beauty, the Ford patient as a mule. Finally, past Adrianople, we worked our way across a bare, waterless, open plain; trucks and buses had worn down the winding track, there were many stones, there was little bread, and, though we managed only eight kilometres an hour, we were glad to make any headway at all. But before us the future road's yellow bed sped arrow-straight to the horizon, and the engineers' white tents shone; hundreds of workers, men, children and grandfathers, had been mobilized. On the barren roadside patient horses and oxen carts waited, crowded together in the midday heat; our automobile seethed, balked at insurmountable gullies and holes, nearly ran out of breath. And yet—work was underway in the new Turkey, and past Lüleburgaz it was indeed the dreamt-of, the future 'International Road' that carried us with lightning speed towards the sea's cool hazy blues and the walls of Byzantium . . .

Enough of the roads: we resolved not to bore readers at home with the workaday worries of our automobile. Why did we let ourselves in for it, for roads like *this*? When I first travelled to the East five and a half years ago, sitting in the Orient Express (we've crossed its tracks, and once even passed its hermetic row of cars), the Balkans were a region of melancholy uniformity. But now, at harvest time, we've seen *the borders*. What richness, what dissimilarities, and then again what simple laws, recurring everywhere: bread was baked, fruit harvested, the hay brought in and cattle herds grazed in the Simplon, on the plain of Treviso, on the Danube (where they called it 'Dunav') and on the hills of European Turkey. The first evening, in the village of Simplon, we spent our last Swiss rappen at the baker's for a round loaf of rye bread with beautiful patterns pressed into its dark crust: a scorpion, constellations and letters. We ate the first piece of this Swiss bread in Piedmont for breakfast in front of our dew-soaked tent, while all around the Italian farmers went to work with shouldered scythes; we chewed the last crust in Bulgaria, just before the Turkish border, where they have wheat, roses and strawberries, corn and tomatoes, but no black bread. We'd eaten many kinds of bread in the meantime. In Italy, the farmers' wives complained a bit and showed us a few grain kernels in their rough hands: 'This is what we have to make coffee from now.'

In Slovenia, at an inn in the village of Kostanjevica, once called 'Landstrass' in German, we were served Viennese coffee, rich milk and fresh 'Kipfel' rolls for breakfast. The landlady also complained a bit in pidgin German: this was once Old Austria, and when the lads went off to the military they came back as 'gentlemen'; Empress Maria Theresa owned a castle in Landstrass where she had coins struck. No trace of it remains in the overgrown park; the Turks destroyed it. What reason is there to complain? The woman edifies us: back then, in the good old days, they belonged to a great empire and had a splendid imperial residence. Even if the roads in Kostanjevica are the same for the Empress' calèches, our automobile, and the Yugoslavian farmers' haywagons, back then the German speakers were the elite . . . And today? We learn that Germans, colonists settled by Maria Theresa, emigrants and others, live as far south as Serbia; in the former garrison towns, the waiters speak German; in Zagreb, it's the market women. And many of these Germans would think it better to belong to a great empire once again. Hapsburg is no more, and so it happens, in the village of Klostar with its beautiful

monastery buildings and its white, unmistakably
Austrian Baroque church, that an entire school class, the
teacher at the fore, greets us with 'Heil Hitler' . . . But
an old farmwoman asks us as we rest in the shade of her
cherry tree: 'My dear sirs,[1] is it true that that Hitler
man's going to come all the way down here?' She emi-
grated from her Bohemian homeland ('the Bohemians
went to Slovenia the way the Slovenians went to
America'), she has to work hard, but she has food, and
she wants to be left in peace . . . Yes, they have food in
Yugoslavia: what abundance, the farmland, pastures and
woods in the hill country past the Italian border, the
vast, rippling fields on the Danube and up to the gates
of Belgrade; and the farmers have splendid teams of
horses, spirited, slender Hungarian dapple-greys to draw
their hay and grain wagons. The men are dressed in
white under colourful vests, and the women wear
embroidered blouses and wide, swaying skirts. This is
how we see them in the evening, coming home from
the fields to villages where flocks of geese cackle by a
tepid village pond. Orient? Occident? The Austrian
atmosphere is gone, no more white Baroque churches
on green hills—let's just call it blessed farmland.

---

1 The German word, 'Herrschaften', is generally used to address
men or mixed company. According to Maillart, several times during the journey Schwarzenbach was 'delighted' to be mistaken for
a man (see Ella Maillart, *The Cruel Way*, London: Virago Press,
1986).

The Bulgarian border: almost a defile, a very narrow valley, and behind it mountains. The road is under construction, so we take a detour and, just beyond the huge, lonely border sign, plunge into a blaze of evening colour: red earth, a mountain stream, green pastures, white cattle and bare slopes. That already has an Asiatic look, when the sunny side of the hill is black and bare of vegetation but the shady side resembles an oasis with water and dark greenery! A few days later, past Sofia, we drive through the famous 'Valley of Roses' towards Plovdiv or Phillippopolis and find not only wild rose fields, the purple flood of lavender, mild air filled with sweet fragrance, but utterly different villages. Vestiges of old Turkey, men in pantaloons and colourful turbans, shy women veiled in black from the head to the trousers gathered at their bare ankles—Mohammedan women. The next day we see them working like slaves under the supervision of an imperious 'patron' who stacks the filled boxes at the side of the road. Do these shy and clearly downtrodden creatures really belong to the same people as the dignified, friendly farmwomen who sat spinning on the thresholds of their village cottages, and the singing girls in their red skirts?

All at once the land turns bleak. On the right flows the Maritsa; beyond it is Greece. But we are approaching a new border. By the stony road, the Turkish flag flutters in the evening sky.

Of all the names that linger in my memory after a long journey, this one is dearest to me. Perhaps because it sounds so Greek, blithe as a swelling paean to carefree days spent on lovely shores? Perhaps because it came at the beginning and now belongs to a long-ago, glorified time— for the journey had just begun, I had just left behind Yugoslavia's vineyards and farming villages, Bulgaria's fields of strawberries and roses, its ochre mountains and the needle-thin minarets of Edirne, had not yet grown used to the shifting sky of the Balkan lands, and already Stamboul was mirrored in the Bosporus!

That was not even a first, preliminary goal, not by far—I recognized the humped roofs of the bazaar, the rising sea of houses and the damp alleys of Vera, the sprawl-ing splendour of the Hagia Sophia and the Süleimaniye, and I heard the surging noise of the cramped metropolis and ate the fried fish and sugared fruits I had tasted once before. Everything had been once before! Everything was mirrored as in a glittering scabbard, the white bridges milling with people, the gently rocking steamships, the gulls, and at last the city wall, lonely in the golden twilight, olives and olive groves at its foot. I felt I must not lose myself in these sights, it was too familiar—and nothing would have stopped me from renting a room on one of the winding streets in Beyoğlu which climb the banks of the river, from sitting at the window, one storey above the street's hollow noise, and gazing down listlessly day after day until evening came. But I could easily do the maths: I'd been on the road just a few days, had only just bought a round loaf of black bread from the village baker at the Simplon Pass, only just eaten the last piece of it, past the Turkish border, by the road, as the first beguiling, untouchable mosque towers appeared against the tender white sky; I'd only just slept on the bank of the Danube, in the shelter of yellow grain fields, only just driven towards a little white Baroque church on the pastoral meadow horizon, passing ox carts, lightly trotting horse teams and a singing procession of farmers' children beneath baldachins and fluttering flags. Only yesterday, from rust-red cliffs near Trieste, I saw the sea, spumy blueness! As I had no particular goal, no wish even to halt some day, come to a rest, greet a paradise on earth, all that meant little to me— slowly a long-seen horizon drew near, church tower and field's edge sank away, flags flickered out, bells faded, the women wore different headscarves and swaying skirts; instead of grazing white cattle I saw sluggish, greasily gleaming water buffalo lying in the warm mud under a bridge; the openness of summer hills and fields was gone, a narrow road passed along the side of a romantic valley cloaked in yellow, rust-brown and violet shadows, into the midst of nameless mountains.

And why should I have known their names! Once on the road, you forget all your thirst for learning, knowing no goodbyes and no regrets, not asking whence and whither. At most the watch dial lets you calculate that time has moved forward an hour or two, meaning you've already made it quite far eastwards. Every day it is more impossible to turn back, nor do you want to now. To tear your clothes, admit that you've gone too far, that you're like a beggar in this strange land, a child without a bed, a priest without a church, a singer without a voice—that you demand shelter, fear you are living in vain? That you want to make amends, make up for what you've missed?

None of us know what we live by—how can we miss something, then, and regret it? In Stamboul, when I arrived very tired late in the evening and the ancient arch of the city gate closed over me, the pavement echoed, oil lamps lighted the street of the bazaar, and at last the glimmering night water of the Bosporus flowed past in ceaseless gliding silence—then, surely, I could have breathed easy and believed for a moment that I had arrived at some kind of destination and had honestly earned this thousandfold fanfare of reunion. But terrible doubts would soon have taken hold: was this really the true, the ultimate place? In my dreams I would have seen the domes of other cities, and when I woke I would have sought their sonorous names on signposts and maps. The journey demands no decisions of us and does not confront our conscience with a single choice to make us guilty and penitent, humble and defiant; soon we despair in all justice and think this life is meant as a labyrinth for us, an ill-fated trial. Departure is liberation—O one and only freedom left us!—and demands only undaunted, daily renewed courage . . .

And so I went about Stamboul like a sleepwalker, unwilling to give in to the visible and tangible familiarity all around, always gazing across the rising sea of roofs to the Asian shore. There another world began, the bare hills of Anatolia, a procession like frozen waves, there greater winds blew, the human voice died away, glossy herds grazed on immeasurable pastures, there the smoke of burnt offerings passed eastwards from steppe to steppe, on to the slant-eyed nomads of Turkistan and onward to the Yellow Sea—there was the threshold I had to cross . . .

That was long ago. The beginning of a great journey has become a gentle, untroubled memory, like a dream you need not fear and do not lose. O memory! Steaming furrows, golden hills—and the hymns which have faded forever, which no longer hurt, no longer move the heart.

Since then names have become mountains, Ararat rose snow-covered from cloud banks, the mighty Hindu Kush was like bronze, in the desert of Turkistan the cold surged with deadly breath, with the swiftness of the famous white-muzzled horses; it took one's words away.

What is left me of that terrible solitude?

Therapia lies as far behind as the isles of childhood. Everything has been said once before, everything surmounted; I want to cover my face now and be silent. If I invoke this name and love it nonetheless, perhaps it is that nothing encumbers it—for it came at the beginning—and nothing clings to it except, carried by faint evening winds and already blown away again, the smell of raspberries, many baskets of them, freshly picked, for sale at the little harbour; the water, saturated and soothed by moonlight, slapped sleep-drunk against the wall, in gardens rising from terrace to terrace leaves stirred and torchlight trickled— for an hour the Bosporus was the paradise never asked for—but already, with jubilant birds and departing fishing boats, the day began to dawn.

If only I could convey the root and route of this journey now ended! With all the surmounted trials, dangers, magics, indelible things—and lie once more on the gently curving bay of Bandra, rest my eyes in the pastel of sea and sky, the sinking horizon. Once more! Convey the comfort of early morning! But I've forgotten everything, even the last hour. Only let me open my eyes to the rapturous encounter . . .

TREBIZOND:
FAREWELL TO THE SEA

A bright young engineer warned us in Istanbul: 'Two women alone who speak no Turkish, you intend to drive from Trabzon straight through the Anatolian backcountry to Iran? You may have no trouble at all, but you may have enough to put you off travel for the rest of your lives . . .' What kind of trouble? The road that's still under construction? It can't be worse than the stretch between Edirne and Lüleburgaz! No place to stay? We'll camp and cook our risotto ourselves. The police? Our passports are in order, and we know we can't take photos in military zones. The engineer shrugged his shoulders: 'The military zones shift, no one knows the details. And not long ago they arrested German spies.'

We aren't spies. We have little use for soldiers or fortifications. But why isn't the road finished yet? 'Don't forget, like his great predecessor Kemal Atatürk, our president is a soldier first and foremost. We need railways before we need roads. Besides, we don't have oil like our neighbour Iran, but we do have coal.'

For now we're gliding down the Bosporus on the white, softly churning steamship *Ankara*, and so lovely is the waterway between green, sloping shores that one struggles to recall the name's very different significance, a grave one, in the great game of war and peace. And despite the sometimes Asiatic bleakness of the hills, the Black Sea feeds from the air and light, the colour and gaiety of the

Mediterranean. The steamship moors off little harbours, off Inebolu and Sinop, off Samsun and Giresun; each time a whole flotilla of heavy fishing boats puts out to sea to meet us, the lads bracing their bare feet against the bench in front of them and rowing as if their lives depended on it; porters, cherry- and bread-sellers climb aboard; in a few minutes, the foredeck of the elegant steamship has been turned into a marketplace and our Ford serves as a display case and a kiosk, a merchant sitting on the running board with his round, flat breads and a boy cheerfully hawking pink ice cream from the luggage rack. The crowd jostles, the humble crowd of our 'steerage' passengers, farmers in old Turkish trousers, an old man in a turban, girls with stockings and skimpy European dresses bought in Istanbul, women shuffling by in loose slippers and baggy pants, hiding their faces behind a tip of the headscarf, and countless filthy children. They live between the bales of goods, the cranes and our automobile, they live on a bit of bread and fruit, they live patiently, knocked about, glad to find enough space for their quilt.

We left Istanbul on 20 June, and on the 23rd, early in the morning, the steamship anchors off the white town of Trabzon. How on earth will they unload our car, I wonder, and the method is unique indeed! They lay cushions of straw beneath the wheels, and then a crane lifts the bucking car over the railing and lowers it into a boat rowed by two men, where the front wheels land on a bench. Barely an hour later the car is standing more or less unscathed in the blazing sun on the quay of Trabzon, and we jolt along the steep alleys of the once-magnificent capital of the Komnenoi.

Little is left of its splendour, a few Byzantine churches and in the gaping ravines the remains of fortifications, yellow towers and walls. And now we're looking not for traces of history but for the office of the Hochstrasser export and import company, which chiefly buys and ships hazelnuts from the area around Trabzon. An old Swiss firm—and a Swiss expatriate, Herr Vonmoos, receives us into his friendly care.

We have no time to stay in Trabzon. Tempting though it would be to gaze out upon the sea's marvellously velvet-blue expanse, to take some part in the small life of this small city with bazaar stands spilling cherries, wild straw-berries, large tomatoes and countless kinds of vegetables, with lush, green countryside and white villas built before the war by the Greeks who settled this coast. We are seeing all this for the last time.

In the afternoon we head out, up the valley. You feel it at once: this is a farewell. This valley is green still, and cooled by the sea air. Cattle in good pastures, hazel bushes, small fields on steep slopes, and everywhere, beneath leafy trees, ancient Greek chapels. As darkness falls we enter a conifer forest, the valley narrows to a gorge, and dense fog blocks the view back, the last view of the sea that Xenophon glimpsed from this height. We are following his path in the opposite direction. And already we've climbed to more than 2,000 metres, to the top of Zigana Pass; it's cold, but not dark yet. We see a magnificent panorama, range upon range, a sea of brown and barren mountains, Asiatic landscape, Asiatic grandeur.

No more Greek chapels, no hazel bushes and fruit trees. We stop in the first town after the top of the pass, Gümüşhane, where trucks are parked outside the illuminated 'restaurant' of the building described to us as a hotel. We are led up the narrow stairs and a kerosene lamp is placed in the room, bare but for three iron bed frames with heavy quilts sewn into not very clean white covers. Downstairs in the lokanta we're given eggs to eat, and a soup of sour milk, herbs, lots of fat. Ella [Maillart] eats a piece of liver she thinks was fried in kerosene. At the next table, unshaven men sit over raki, one of them an architect, another a road engineer; these are the professions the new Turkey needs. 'You're driving to Erzurum and onward? You'll see, the road is partly finished, and there's construction everywhere . . .'

A vast land lies before us. We've left the coast behind, the gentle air, the beautiful sky that reminded us of the Mediterranean and joined us to it still. At night—we locked the door with a short chain and a hook attached to the threshold—a policeman demands entry and takes away our passports. We are no longer in a free country. The police want to know where we spent our nights. Will we still be able to camp where we like? And as the headlights of the trucks blaze up outside and the motors start with a roar, we think wistfully of Yugoslavia's gentle landscape, our camp on the bank of the Danube, under trees . . .

MOUNT ARARAT

I don't know how long I sat on the roof of Bayazid Fortress, gazing over from that craggy height to the mountain of Ararat. It was a splendid sight! Hour followed hour, and the wind, blustering in the cliffs and hurling itself back down onto the plain again like a rallying legion, was the same wind as in the sprawling, fortified hills of Erzurum and early in the morning over the young Euphrates that springs forth in a bare lunar valley. Day and night the same wind, and again in the morning, and year after year—could you still breathe, recover yourself, could you ever again turn your gaze from that summit—crowned by eternal snow, shrugging off billowing banners of cloud—and bend it towards an olive branch? Get up, make your bed and go out to find the people at work again on the arid plain? They were building the new road to Tabriz, laying beds of rock and building bridges, draining swamps and erecting, at the foot of the ageless fortress, the future Bayazid, a town of clay and corrugated iron. There they lived, young engineers, workers, farmers, Turks, Russians, people with no homeland, officials and adventurers, pioneers without women, and had every sip of drinking water brought up from the far-off mountain gorges. Not so far, on the nearly grassless plain, a rusty track ran like a vein of water through the desert sand and a few old locomotives lay like animals brought to their knees: the remains of the strategic railway built by the Russians in the World War. A new road, a new railway—I heard the clatter of heavy steamrollers on the gravel and the tromp of countless yokes of oxen smoothing the way. Already it ran like a white arrow towards the Persian border, over rocky ridges, past Kurdish villages and the still-smoking ruins of Armenian churches, straight across the parched, fissured bed of the Flood. And not an olive tree on the road! The two tame Babylonian lions dead of old age, the round-crouped wild donkeys gone astray in their hunger for freedom! Herds of greasily gleaming water buffalo replaced the elephants, lying indolently in the mud beneath the new bridges; at a great distance, a great height, I saw the blissful circles turned by the little falcon that dealt the grey dove the death blow. In a village beyond the border—it lay surrounded by tree-lined canals in Persia's lonely, leprous yellow expanse, a shadowless blue mountain at its edge like a mirage of Ararat—there, they told me, the patriarch Noah lies buried in a vineyard.

We didn't even stop there. Nor in the clay-coloured Kurdish villages amid fields of grain in the ear, nor on the saddle-shaped rise, the border between Turkey and Persia, where Anatolia's rain fronts and massed clouds suddenly give way, the slate-grey rocks and scrubby steppe grass of the highlands fall behind and from one moment to the next the eye must accustom itself to the airy dome, the evanescent blue of the Persian sky, the plain of a strange country, blinding, quivering with light, hardly bounded at all by the blue of blurring mountains. Since then, the Bayazid region was struck by the great earthquake of autumn 1939. Atatürk's successor was shown in the newspaper shaking the hands of widows, orphans and the homeless. By that time Europe was already at war.

Surely the fortress of Bayazid collapsed, towers and walls sinking tipsily like air-filled sails, the village hearth fires were smothered, the terraced gardens covered with ash. And the child who followed me through the alleys, so doggedly, but at a distance—slain too in the hail of rock debris.

I wonder now at the notes I took during the journey. I've forgotten most of the names. The legends I collected— I don't even want to tell them. The inviting gardens, the peach trees and the transfigured evening landscapes, all seem covered by ash. We spent a night in the cliff village of Maku and just barely survived a terrible storm. Lightning-lit as if by fireworks, a flood burst from the overhanging cliff wall, within seconds the village lane had turned into a streambed, then a field of rubble; only the shattered roofs of the bazaar showed amid the piled-up blocks of the rockslide.

The next morning, the young officer overseeing the clearance work walked with us across the terraces of Maku to the foot of the highest cliffs where stood the victory inscription of Nadir Shah, who once wrested this village from a band of robbers. Drops of water issued from the cool, shady vault and fell singly, slowly through the blue air like shimmering beads. I remember it vividly: the gentle, dazing veil of earthly dew, and how I sat in the Emir's little garden shivering, exhausted from the heat of the steep climb, and a young farmwoman raised the water jug to my lips. For such are we, we delight in beads, the sea's blue, a peaceful hour amid raging infernos, we look unseeing at fields of rubble so that we all may learn the same prayer: Lord, help us to eke out our lives . . .

A few days later I saw Mount Damavand for the last time. I don't want to argue. Ararat was bigger, resting broader and more surely in the Anatolian plain and raising its snow-covered peak more singularly from the scattering clouds. Its name comes down from ancient, pious times; the dear animal-friendly legend of Noah's Ark still lodges there on high, unmistakable, and the young Euphrates foams between birch banks.

Damavand is a heavenly body. I want to forget its name at last—but see it again, see it one more time!

That evening camel bells and columns of dust enveloped me, my throat was parched, my eyes were nearly blinded. Then in the bright night rose a cloud that I took for one of those visions of the East, a mirage. I saw it dissolve into the strangely clear horizon—there, a striated pyramid, stood the extinct volcano, a pain-filled, deeply moving sight: permanence.

Part Two

THE STEPPE

It's long ago now, two months or two and a half, and already it belongs to the past. And yet it was the same summer whose end I am experiencing in Kabul, the capital of Afghanistan, and part of the same journey that has brought me here by way of many borders, capitals and stations of all kinds. The Grisons license number and the little Swiss cross on my Ford prove to me if necessary that everything has happened according to plan and just as I find it recorded in my diary entries. And sometimes it is necessary. Perhaps my sense of reality is not very highly developed, perhaps I lack a sound and reassuring instinct for the solid facts of our earthly existence; I can't always tell memories from dreams, and often I mistake dreams, coming to life again in colours, smells, sudden associations, with the eerie secret certainty of a past life from which time and space divide me no differently and no better than a light sleep in the early hours.

'Our life is like a journey . . .'[2]—and so the journey seems to me less an adventure and a foray into unusual realms than a concentrated likeness of our existence: residents of a city, citizens of a country, beholden to a class or a social circle, member of a family and clan and entangled by professional duties, by the habits of an 'everyday life' woven from all these circumstances, we often feel too

---

2 From the 'Beresinalied', a patriotic song recalling the sacrifices of Swiss troops who fought for Napoleon at the Battle of Berezina.

secure, believing our house built for all the future, easily induced to believe in a constancy that makes ageing a problem for one person and each change in external circumstances a catastrophe for another. We forget that this is a process, that the earth is in constant motion and that we too are affected by ebbs and tides, earthquakes and events far beyond our visible and tangible sphere: beggars, kings, figures in the same great game. We forget it for our would-be peace of mind, which then is built on shifting sand. We forget it so as not to fear. And fear makes us stubborn: we call reality only what we can grasp with our hands and what affects us directly, denying the force of the fire that's sweeping our neighbour's house, but not yet ours. War in other countries? Just twelve hours, twelve weeks from our borders? God forbid—the horror that sometimes seizes us, you feel it too when reading history books, time or space, it doesn't matter what lies between us and it.

But the journey ever so slightly lifts the veil over the mystery of space—and a city with a magical, unreal name, Samarkand the Golden, Astrakhan or Isfahan, City of Rose Attar, becomes real the instant we set foot there and touch it with our living breath. The pavement of Damascus echoes under our feet, the hills of Erzurum glow in the evening light, the minarets of Herat loom at the end of the plain. But a cholera epidemic detains us in Iran, and what just now was a fleeting vision, a breathing spell, becomes an episode, a segment of lived life. In Kabul we form friendships, make ourselves at home; we know the Russian who bakes European bread and Gulam Haidar who sells fountain pens, airmail envelopes and Veramon. Already we have our daily habits, find our way home in the dark, and ultimately it is only an accident that we won't spend the rest of our lives here: here or elsewhere, on the shore of the Caspian Sea, for instance, where the climate is hellish, the caviar dirt-cheap and malarial fever free of charge.

Did we once study the customs and mores of foreign peoples? Well and good, but we didn't learn how the Afghan wraps his turban, and we didn't know how the daily pilaf tastes in a country where every day you get rice and mutton to eat and tea to drink, and never a drop of alcohol. On a journey the face of reality changes with the mountains and rivers, with the architecture of the buildings, the layout of the gardens, with the language, the skin colour. And yesterday's reality burns on in the pain of parting; the day before yesterday's is a finished episode, never to return; what happened a month ago is a dream, a past life. And at last you realize that the course of a life contains nothing but a limited number of such 'episodes', that a thousand and one accidents determine where we can build our house at last—but the peace of our poor minds is a precious good of freedom that you should not chase, nor haggle over, nor should you bargain for it with the dictators who can set fire to our houses, trample our fields and spread cholera overnight.

Appalling uncertainty . . .? Appalling only when we fail to look it in the eyes. But the journey that many may take for an airy dream, an enticing game, liberation from daily routine, freedom as such, is in reality merciless, a school that accustoms us to the inevitable course of events, to encounters and losses, blow upon blow. 'The journey

to Kabul' that is traceable on the map, if only in broad out-
lines, and calculable in kilometres, if only roughly, is
already a finely woven tapestry in my memory, woven hour
by hour from living breath, sweat and blood, and lost
beyond recall, for time wears seven-league boots now that
far from my path an event has intervened—the war—
ambushing me and no doubt most of my fellows like the
blind and the deaf.

It's two months ago now, or two and a half. This same
summer, late July, and I'd left the Iranian plateau and
driven down from the Firuzkuh Pass into Mazandaran's
dense primaeval forests, its humid jungles, its flooded rice
paddies covered by mosquito swarms, to the pale blue coast
of the Caspian hemmed by mournful dunes. Fertile,
melancholy land—familiar from early life, from dreams
and the memories of recent years—where the Shah had
cotton mills built, model plantations and tobacco sheds.
The farmers, living in a stupor of poverty from the harvest
of their rice fields, were put to work in the factories, supplied with quinine, tea replaced rice, native silk cocoons
were processed; in the fishing village of Mashhad-i-Sar[3] a
Palace Hotel was built, Swiss hotel directors and master
dyers, silk weavers and cooks were hired. Children are
forced to work twelve-hour shifts, the ten-year-olds earning half a kran or about fifteen rappen a day, the older ones
two krans a day, but at night school the most gifted are
trained to perfection as weavers and spinners, even over-
seers and many other things.

---

3 This is the town's historic name; from 1927 it was known as
Babolsar (Maillart has it as Babol-Sar; see *The Cruel Way*, p. 89).

A Swiss man put me up that night; his wife made us coffee while we sat on the terrace in the sultry air and he told me about the country and the people and the blessings of working for progress: much had changed since my last visit four years ago. The next morning I left Mazandaran, the Caspian fell behind, the jungle opened up. No more thatched roofs, no rice paddies, no animal skulls on fences. Then the tobacco fields ended and with them the Shah's lands. Then the cornfields the farmers had been left with. Pastures still—and somewhere, in a hill's gentle hollow, a village, trees, bread. A blond-bearded man walked down the road in high boots, a hoe over his shoulder. I stopped the car; the blue-eyed man replied tersely, in Russian: yes, he'd come from over there, from Russia, with other muzhiks. They couldn't live back home any more, the Red Guard had taken their last cow and the crosses and icons from their cottages. Now they had a new village here in Iran. There was black bread and honey; did we want to buy some? But there was no navigable road to the village, and the Russian didn't mind when we parted and I continued on my straight path: eastwards, towards a wide horizon.

The air was thin and dry. A hot wind rose. No more trees now, no grass, no field, no village, no cottage, no fence, no water. The ground turned yellow. Suddenly the pale sky sank like a heavy canopy, smothering all life beneath it, and went violet and sulphurous yellow, rust-brown, fire-red in evening's rapid fall—a beautiful spectacle, but dire as a vision from the *Divine Comedy*. And now I knew what books and map had so inadequately taught me: that I had left the tropical basin of the Caspian and entered the

Turkmen Steppe—the beginning of the vast steppes and deserts that stretch through all of Central Asia to the Far East. And I saw this place for the first time. Home of the nomads, the black tents, the yurts. But in Iran the programme of progress had forced the nomads to settle down, robbing the tribes of their leaders and already almost stamping them out. And the carpets of the Pend[4] and the Tekke Turkmens, their colourful saddlebags and tent bands, their swift horses? To my left, on a horizon now extinct and leaden, I saw a few wretched goat-felt tents and the oddly majestic silhouettes of a few gaunt camels. A dog barked. And from the Caspian, from the west, white vultures came with slow wing-beats. That was all. The steppe sprawled in silence, desolation, the heat was deadly, the night and this 'beginning of Asia' merged into a dark vision. And before me, straight ahead, unquestionably, then, at the end of my path, loomed the Gunbad-i-Qabus. The Mongol tower, gigantic and austere, and I did not ask whether the glass coffin still hangs beneath its peaked roof, as the steppe legend has it. This sufficed: the overwhelming monument to the man who had not feared the poverty and grandeur of the steppe, so alien to all human measures. I breathed deep and tried, despite all, to salute life . . .

---

4 'Pendinischen Turkmenen' in the German. Perhaps a reference to the village of Penjdeh or Panjdeh in Turkistan.

They huddled inside the tower, a clutch of old men, not daring to raise their heads, as though afraid of hitting a low prison ceiling.[5] And yet the tower was immeasurably tall, a Mongol tomb, the looming landmark of the steppe. In its marvellous vault, a bold and flawless construction of clay brick, the country's sons believed they still glimpsed the glass coffin that seven hundred years ago a mighty khan had suspended there on silver chains so that he might be safe from grave-robbers and enemies.

The Gunbad-i-Qabus! Comparable to no other edifice, not the Pyramids erected by enslaved peoples; not the pillars of Persepolis or the turquoise minarets of Herat, grand testaments to great rulers; still less the crusader cathedrals, warlike fortresses; nor the golden domes of Najaf and Mashhad, paid for by pious pilgrims. For this tower is lonely, lonely—destined for no renown, consecrated to no devotions and no purpose. The steppe peoples know it as they know the wind from the Caspian and the caravan tracks, and they praise it, the guidepost, consoler, son of

---

5 In Maillart's account, 'There was nothing inside the tower' (*The Cruel Way*, p. 93). But 'When she visited the Gumbad-i-Kabus a few years ago, my friend Irene found in that great tower many tribal chiefs being kept as hostages till their sons returned from Soviet Russia' (ibid., 91). If Maillart was not mistaken, perhaps this passage should be read as an imaginative elaboration of her anecdote rather than an actual encounter between Schwarzenbach and the prisoners.

the heavens. Migrating birds skim its top, camels graze at the foot of the hill, and as far as the eye can see this is nomad territory, the realm of black tents.

Now the tower has been occupied by dutiful officials, educated, wearing uniforms, giving orders, requisitioning, collecting taxes in the name of the authorities, law and order! And progress!

The old men in the tower are prisoners and understand little of the legal wording. But they remember other days; they owned weapons then, and swift horses, the steppe thundered beneath unshod hooves, and all around, in the dust-shimmering evening light, great freedom spread, a sea of golden waves! How joyful their sons were, growing up!

At that the poor old men fall silent, but their lips keep moving anxiously. For their boys are to blame, their pride! The gendarme writes down the names, the imprisoned fathers nod patiently, almost tenderly: 'Yes, Ali Asker, that's my son, and Jakub, that's my youngest, good-looking, a brave rider, the women loved him.'

The man in uniform grows impatient. And writes, writes down like a scribe and Pharisee—the old men have long since fallen silent. There it stands confirmed: their sons, joy and pride of their old age, Ali Asker and Jakub and many more, members of the Pend Turkmen tribe, have fled across the border to the Soviet Union, evading taxes, military service and the new laws, refusing to settle down, invoking unwritten grazing rights; they are declared to have forfeited their herds and tents, they are declared guilty and must pay a fine of so and so many tomans and rials to the state, *the state*!

'But you, ill-fated fathers, shall be held responsible and detained until dark-haired Jakub returns and repents . . .'

The old men have not learned to read and write. Hands guided, they sign their names to their offence.

Soon no more black tents will be seen on the Turkmen Steppe, no colourful saddlebags, rugs, tent bands, no unshod horses. Instead cotton fields, tobacco sheds, textile mills, schools and hospitals, barracks.

In a village near the Russian-Iranian border—the shore of the Caspian lay pale in the west, in the east the horizon of the Turkmen Steppe—I met two blond fellows who offered to patch my car's flat tyre. They brought me tea and melons, laid out their tools and went to work. They were Russians, Ivan and Piotr. 'You've come from Gunbad-i-Qabus, the Mongol tower?' they asked me. They had never seen the tower, but they knew: there the border was near, the border of Soviet Russia, their homeland.

'Are you refugees?' I asked.

'But of course, refugees, religious Russians. Back there they wanted to make us renounce our faith, they wanted to put us in a cotton kolkhoz with miserable, half-starved nomads. So we ran away.'

'And here?'

Ivan and Piotr have malarial fever and live in an old caravanserai with a samovar and a golden icon. They're in a bad way, homesick.

But they know their craft; diligent, dripping with sweat, they mount my patched wheel. Amiably they wish me a good journey. They're so friendly, so artless, so piously resigned to their fate! 'On to Afghanistan?' they ask. 'Perhaps it's different there, better, a free land, a promised land?' And they wave . . .

On towards the east! Towards other skies! But all the while I drive along the edge of the steppe, knowing that this is the great, the eternal border between Iran and Turan, between Herat and Samarkand, between the Hindu Kush, the Pamir and the bank of the Oxus—the border between the highlands that rear up before blessed India and the sea coasts and the immeasurable expanses of Asia.

Today this means: the Russian border with Iran and Afghanistan. It means: the Soviet Socialist Republics of Turkmenistan, Uzbekistan, Tajikistan. In the midst of the Pamir lies Stalinabad, airplanes land, veins of tin are mined; in the midst of the huge, desert-like steppe, canals are dug and fields are farmed; the Emir of Bukhara lives as a blind refugee in an Afghan village near Kabul; his loyalists, nomads, farmers, feudal lords, follow him across the Amu Darya,[6] taking their sheep herds with them. A flood of refugees streams across the border to Afghanistan, is absorbed, settled down—land in the Sistan Desert, land in the Hindu Kush, pastures, state-run cotton fields and sugar factories in Afghan Turkistan.

Wherever you turn, progress is on the march, organization is called for, the state becomes all-powerful, the people learn to read and write, are given civil rights, pay taxes, serve in the military, build roads and set up artillery.

From modernized, progressive Iran nameless nomads flee across the steppe that is their home, not knowing what

---

6 Another name for the Oxus River.

awaits them on the other side, in Soviet Russia. From the Asian Soviet Republics thousands flee southwards over the Oxus and are taken in by the Afghan state, sent to new factories, paid, settled, incorporated into the new proletariat. They submit, and one, a blond-bearded Russian from Bukhara employed by the new German-built power plant of Pul-i-Khumri, tells me sullenly: 'There's work here, the work gets paid. What more do you want?'

It's not ambition that drives them, not hope that spurs them. But the poor, the prisoners get used to many things, to everything, clinging tenaciously to wretched life. For there are laws, fatalities—and to rebel, to venture the needless attempt, to die the futile death is given to few. May they be granted, then, a stay to stay out their time!

But on both sides of the border, far from the new roads, lie untouched fields, summer pastures, bathed in gold and night-clear starlight. There I still found the herds and nomad tents of free, armed, hospitable men.

Mashhad lies behind us. Let us forget the city, over whose
new, straight streets and narrow, roofed, twilit bazaar lanes
the golden dome of Imam Reza's tomb shines like a bell
lowered from the sky's fixed blue, like a heavenly body
spinning resplendent at noon. Let us forget the immortal
blue of the Goharshad Mosque, the crushing heat in the
courts that seem to sing with the harmony of colours and
forms; let us forget the darkness and the mirrored splendour inside the shrine, and the moaning and weeping of
emaciated pilgrims, Shiites from all parts of Asia who have
dreamt for decades of kissing the sarcophagus grating and
have crossed deserts, endured hardships to step barefoot
on the marble floor today, to watch the opening of the
doors, fourteen silver and two gold. At that they fall
sobbing to their knees, with harsh cries of exhaustion and
hysterical desire they cling to the iron bars behind which,
in the dark, the Imam rests amid mouldering carpets,
turbans, votive offerings and holy scriptures.[7] But outside,
all around the sprawling mosque, the craftsmen, copper-
and silversmiths, saddlers and tailors, sit in tiny booths like
cages, and the merchants haggle in round vaults stuffed

---

7 According to Maillart, the two were not allowed inside the
tomb-chamber; Schwarzenbach viewed it through a peephole,
while Maillart described her visit inside two years previously (see
ibid., 106). This passage seems to reflect Maillart's own descrip-
tion of the chamber from within.

with dusty carpets, and it's fifty steps down the shaft from the bazaar to the gloom of the cistern; the ragged porters stagger under the weight of leather water bags. Let us forget the city. A mighty wind blows across the road to the east that turns at once into a desert track . . . The scattered straw-yellow fields give way to woeful aridity; from the bare mountains one still sees qanat mounds, built in long rows across the plain, the thirsty crater mouths of subterranean canals sustaining a village, a bit of green around a hive colony of round clay domes cracking in the heat. Or in the courtyard of a fortress-like caravanserai the qanat water fills a cistern, and in the adjoining vaulted room men give us tea and melons.

Yes, people live even here—and Persia has one last surprise in store for us like a parting present to charm a guest. We stop at two in the afternoon in the town of Torbat and look around for shade; in the middle of the intersection of two perpendicular streets is the obligatory round plaza found in all towns of the new Iran, with a police post, a few dried-up flowerbeds, some sand and gravel. Nothing but crumbling clay walls all around, caves, human habitations—but somewhere across the yellow sea of debris there's a gleam of turquoise, and a winding path takes us to the door of a mosque whose remains still conjure up all the splendour and grace of Shah Abbas the Great's day. First a garden, the front court; a pine's broad fan of boughs gives shade, and grass grows—to us, it seems as soft and lush as a carpet. The triangle of a chain in the low gate, a blind man, a guard, a few boys—then, amid bushes, the clay-yellow and alabaster stones of a cemetery, and, looming startlingly into the sky, the high gate, the mihrab, adorned with delicate tendrils of blue and turquoise. Next to it, half-hidden by a wall, the gleaming green-tiled dome of a tomb.

Here, we are told, Shah Abbas ordered the old tomb of a khan destroyed, having taken him for a Sunni, an apostate from the true faith of the Shiites. But he was mistaken. And in penance he vowed to build a new shrine after completing a military campaign.

We would like to lie here in the shade once more, Persian-style, our gaze in the blue, and eat melons. But a policeman dogs our steps; photography is forbidden. He escorts us to the hot courtyard of a 'garage', and we're glad to drink a little tea and escape without further incident. Still nearly a hundred kilometres to the border—and the horizon grows wider and emptier, the wind stronger and hotter, the mountains peter out at the edge of the plain, we cross dry riverbeds. When will evening come, a little coolness? At last a hill, crowned by the clay rectangle of a fortress, a soldier in front in a light-blue uniform. And just past it, in the hollow, the village of Pussusabad[8] or Kariz— the border.

Seven in the evening. We are escorted into a large courtyard and brought tea, cucumbers, grapes, melons, promised that the 'boss' will be woken. From the murky pool that betokens the 'garden' we fetch water for our car's boiling-hot radiator; the formalities take time, the moon looms in the pale grey sky. And we are warned against driving on alone at this hour, into the no man's land . . .

---

8 This name could not be confirmed. Maillart refers to the town as 'Karez' (ibid., p. 111).

But we want to reach the other side, Islam Qala, the first outpost of *Afghanistan*. After so many borders we've touched on, crossed—this time it is *our* border, long anticipated, yearned for. And on the other side, past the swath of desert now veiled in gloom, lies Afghanistan.

What is so important and special about it? Is this the parting of two continents? Will the yellow of the clay change, the hot wind, the aspect of the distant bounding range, will the plains become less endless, the horizons more comforting?

Demarcations have often shifted here. The next larger Afghan city, still 150 kilometres away from us, is *Herat*, the capital of the Timurids, which holds the proudest minarets, monuments as imposing as those of Samarkand. Herat, it's said, divided great Timur's realm into its Indo-Afghan and its Iranian half. From Balkh, ancient Bactria, the roads lead to the Oxus and onward over to Turkistan, onward down to Kandahar, Kabul and India—O magic of names! Still no glimpse of Islam Qala's lonely lights ahead of us, still we grope through the desert, following the telegraph poles, and the thistles rustle beneath our wheels. No tracks at all: for days, perhaps for weeks, no car seems to have come this way, and we recall that the frontier traffic, sparse in any case, has been blocked due to cholera. We are passing between the countries thanks to a few twists of fate, and we call them lucky twists. White birds escort us, vultures sailing on silent wings, and the moon is the same colour. Hasn't it finally turned a bit cooler? The wind comes from the Amu Darya, from Russia—and pillars of sand spin to the south, towards the great desert that reaches to Zainan, Sistan, Baluchistan, all the way to the Persian Gulf, the desert along whose edge we move. We extinguish the light of the odometer . . .

And suddenly I see three white forms in front of me, close enough to touch. White turbans, white teeth, white, fluttering, billowed trousers—and outthrust rifles and harsh cries force me to stop. Dark faces in the car window, the three lads talk away at us all at once, quickly, urgently, and we laugh: 'You'll have to speak French with us, or German.' One tosses his shotgun behind our seats and climbs lighting-quick into the car, an agile young giant. He shows us the way to Islam Qala.

A little later we're lying on our sleeping bags on the floor of a room in one of the border buildings. No tree, I think, no garden, but surely a cistern, and out there in the thistly desert camel herds and black tents? Then: the Silk Road passed this way—is this the route of Marco Polo, of Alexander's soldiers?

Outside our window an Afghan dressed in white lies on a carpet. He reaches out one hand and murmurs, half-asleep: 'Do you have a cigarette?'

Part Three

THE WOMEN OF KABUL

HERAT, 1 AUGUST 1939 . . .

Letters are usually dated, after all, and we've done the
maths several times over and compared our journals: today
is undoubtedly 1 August. But when will this letter reach
home? Will the bonfires be forgotten by then, will the date
seem obsolete and slightly odd in a world accustomed to
radio?[9] Journalists, people who feel called upon to report
things in the newspaper, ought to be quick to the punch,
finding ways and means anytime and everywhere . . . one
might judge. Incidentally, we're not so very far from the
Amu Darya, from the Russian-Turkish border, and on the
other side there's a railway—but what do kilometres and
timetables count for here! In Mashhad, a young Iranian,
hearing that we wanted to continue on to Afghanistan in
our Ford, told me: 'A camel is slower than a horse but it's
surer to reach its destination.' Two days later we bogged
down in the sand on a stretch of the no man's land near the
Iranian-Afghan border posts with not a single tyre track to
be seen. It was only twenty yards of sand, to be precise, but
each metre cost us lots of sweat and nearly half an hour—
we'd have been glad of a yoke of oxen, if not a horse . . .

And so, arriving in Herat today, we'd have every reason for a celebratory bonfire, if only it weren't too hot for
that. A constant, implacable wind blows from the yellow
hills north of the city; we close all the windows to keep the

---

9 1 August is Swiss National Day, often marked by the lighting
of bonfires.

central room of our small and completely unshaded house halfway cool. The wind lasts for a month, the Heratis tell us, and then a pleasant autumn begins. Thus it's better to spend the afternoon sleeping and wait for the evening.

I got up around five in the morning to take the Ford to the master mechanic; the merchants were just opening their stalls, filling baskets with grapes, stacking up pyramids of yellow and pale green melons, pouring milk into gaping sheepskins and sprinkling on a powder and a bit of *mast* from the previous day to ferment the fresh *mast*, their sour milk. Riders trotted towards the centre of town, white turbans fluttered, donkeys brayed and the master, wearing a kula of beautiful grey karakul, opened for me, with the help of his assistants, the gate to his yard, where the wreck of a run-down Chevrolet lay lonely in the early sun. Our car had been through quite a bit, sandstorms, thistly deserts and riverbeds filled with pebblestones; and just yesterday, right outside the house of the 'mudir' we'd visited, I'd driven it off the left side of a treacherous little clay bridge into a rather deep ditch. The master mechanic feels the springs, smiles, and promises to do his best. I watch him for an hour or so—after that, on the way home, it's already almost hot. So we wait for evening. And when the car is ready, maybe we'll drive north and spend the night somewhere in the mountains where there's shade, good water and the nomads' black tents.

The evenings here in Herat are not exactly cool but golden, and the moon floats pale above the edge of the old eroded city walls of yellow clay before sailing off to the blue mountains, the fantastically serrated spurs of the Hindu

Kush. White turbans and dignified kulas fill the lanes of the bazaar, and the streets leading out of the city tremble to the rapid trot of handsome, spirited horses pulling two-wheeled gadis—all heading for the spruce-lined avenue and the garden oasis in the barren hill country. Up there the camels of large caravans jam the roads with a din of bells . . .

A young Pole comes to visit us—the only European in Herat, an engineer hired by the state to build roads and bridges and houses. 'Do you have newspapers?' he asks at once, 'do you know what's going on in the world?' Heavens no, we know as little as he—we were just barely able to figure out the date, for the letter. What's happening in politics? But we've run away from politics! 'Far enough,' the young Pole murmurs, 'far enough!'—and gives me a pack of real English cigarettes. Now I should explain exactly what a present like that means here, at the end of the world. But evening has come, the wind is less fierce, the light less white: we want to go out to the street and stop a gadi, drawn by a dapple-grey, if possible, or a skewbald. Letters have time, time costs nothing in these parts—let's return to the melons and peaches of Afghanistan.

Travelling journalists like to tell each other: 'Spend six weeks in a country, and you'll blithely write a book about it. Stay six months, and you'll struggle to finish a few articles. If you stay six years, you'll have nothing more to say . . .' But the exceptions prove the rule, and the first time, coming from the north, from Turkistan's blazing plain, when I reached the Hindu Kush and crossed its grandiose, historic passes, I was sorely tempted to write a hymn and nothing else. A hymn to its name, for names are more than geographic labels, they're sound and colour, dream and memory, they're mystery, magic—and it's not sobering in the least, it's a miraculous act to rediscover them one day weighed down by the sheen and the shadow, the fire and the cold ash of reality. Pamir, Hindu Kush, Karakorum—just as I did earlier, in the classroom, I stubbornly refused to believe that the names I learnt and read on the map could take form before I'd seen them with my eyes, touched them with my breath, held them as it were in my hands. The simultaneity of near and far confused me; I thought it possible to find the past, the present and the future united in one place, giving it all that life can hold; but I had grave doubts that at any given moment life might reign both here and there, on this side and that side of the seas and mountains. And such doubts, demanding resolution, may have inspired my earliest journeys: I went forth, not to learn what fear was but to test what the names held and feel their magic in the flesh, just as, at the open window, you feel the miraculous power of the sun you'd long seen reflected on distant hills and spread on dewy meadows.

This time it was the Hindu Kush I had to reach, was bound to reach one day, for coming from Persia I'd entered the northern provinces of Afghanistan, heading south for Kabul, the capital—and between the north and the south of this wild country the Hindu Kush rears like a mighty fortress. And I saw its name marked on the English map and took the only possible route: from Herat to Qal`eh-ye Now, from Qal`eh-ye Now to Bala Murghab, to Mana[10] and Andkhoy, and then the ruins of Balkh loomed on the desert's edge, and a sandy track ended at Mazar-i-Sharif, the capital of Afghan Turkistan. It was not much further now, and I should have felt sure of myself. But how long had I been on the road now, and whenever I asked the people would say: 'Nastik ast, bisyar nastik . . .'—'It's near, very near!' On horseback or on foot or with the donkey trot and swaying camel gait of the caravans? A few days' journey, a few hours'? The track might peter out into the sand like the little rivers that strove in vain towards the great Amu Darya, the desert might sprawl in the south as it did in the north, the August heat might last a full hundred and twenty days like the famous north wind of Herat, and this journey along the edge of Turkistan's great lowlands might never come to an end.

One night, I recall, I was stranded with two flat tyres amid the heat-gorged, eerily silent garden walls of a village that seemed to lose itself in ruins and strange clay cliffs, as in the labyrinth of a Dantesque entrance to Hell. The town

10 Presumably Maymana.

was called Tashkurghan, and a few hours later the police chief who had been alarmed escorted my car to the gate of a fairy-tale palace that lay white in the moonlight at the end of a gently and endlessly upsloping garden. Beyond the high garden wall I saw a blue mountain range, prodigious, like part of the night sky, not of this world. There, I thought, there could be neither rock nor grass, no gorges and valleys, no trees, pastures, shepherds' fires, no glaciers, no storms. All was uniform, velvety matter, cloaked in haze, saturated and suffused by moonlight all the way to the fantastically serrated ridge which would surely dissolve to the touch, melding with the milky clouds. I acquiesced in the beautiful vision, rapt, incurious, but the police chief of Tashkurghan had me know: that, to the south, was the first chain of the Hindu Kush . . .

That was a full four months ago, or a little longer. What is left to say? The hymn! The hymn to the end of a moonlit night, to the road that wound through crumbling clay walls, leaving behind the gardens in their agony of pale heat, leading upwards in a long dim dawn through a valley with flat bare slopes to reach Haibak in a sudden, splendid burst of morning light—Haibak, amid young meadows and gentle hills, yellow fields, rippling grain, inviting groves and an old bridge over the river's brisk rush. And next to the bridge cheerful whitebeards sat outside a chaikhana, legs crossed on the straw mat, colourfully trimmed pointed shoes beside them, samovar smoking, and there was green tea, warm Uzbek bread and fragrant melons; the air was cool, and a playful little wind came from the mountains. Later, I recall, there came a pass, and then the hot, humid lowlands of Pul-i-Khumri filled with mosquito swarms, wild ducks and water buffalo. Pul-i-Khumri, where, past the jutting overhang of a hill with Buddhist ruins, the world suddenly changes, amid the malaria-infested wilderness a dam looms, brick kilns, half-completed factory buildings, white houses roofed with corrugated iron and much more besides: tearooms, bazaar stalls, tent colonies, Persian, Russian, German signs, Russian refugees, German engineers. And Uzbeks, Turkmens, Hazara, Tajiks, Afghans, nomads condemned to factory work, farmers pressed into forced labour—the strangest mixture of races and tongues, the new proletariat of a state striving towards civilization. And that in the middle of the Hindu Kush! At the gateway to the province of Badakhshan, famous for its fine, white-muzzled horses, from the Tang Emperors and Genghis Khans to this very day!

Past Pul-i-Khumri the hills turned steeper, the cliffs closed in, gorges gaped, shadows spread. At fantastic heights you glimpsed fiery mountain peaks, a blue banner of sky, while kept captive hour after hour in the dark narrows where the caravans slipped like shadows along the embankment and slant-eyed donkey drivers lit great fires for a long night beneath the cliffs. Morning came and evening came again, tea in Doshi, trout and cold wind in Bulula, black nomad tents, the last Turkmen yurts, the first Afghan tribesmen, long-haired, blazing-eyed, wearing earrings and speaking Pashto. And at last the Shibar Pass, so steep and stark and stupendous that it is sometimes claimed to be the highest automobile road on earth. At any rate it leads across, across to the southern slopes of the Hindu Kush and down into an exquisite valley. Yes, the earth is milder here, and there are villages, there are herds, there's fragrant hay, the great winds are left behind, the breath of the desert is held at bay . . .

That was four months ago, as I said, or a little longer. At the time I thought it was my only, my final encounter with the Hindu Kush, that with each step I left a place, a tuft of grass, a breath of wind, an experience behind me forever. Why do I recite the names of villages, passes, tribes—I forgot them, extinguished them and slipped through my Hindu Kush dream as through twilight, morning fog and high noon's intoxication with the blazing sun. And all this fell behind, I had already taken leave when I turned onto the plain of Kabul, the weeks passed uncounted, autumn came.

Then one morning I found myself on the road to Turkistan again.[11] Setting out in the last hour of the night, I saw the distant mountains loom in the dawn, blue, cold, snow-crowned and splendid to behold. 'The Hindu Kush a second time,' I realized—but now all the names counted and stayed put, I discovered more valleys, more peaks, and it elated me to find, towards noon, an orchard where I'd slept once, and on the square of Ghorband, surrounded by little tearooms, a young merchant who'd sold me grapes and melons then, and now counted off 120 walnuts on his

---

11 After parting ways with Maillart in Kabul in October 1939, Schwarzenbach travelled back north to spend three weeks in Kunduz assisting the Délégation Archéologique Française en Afghanistan.

fingers for one Afghani. But though my memory was tenderly roused by lovely vistas once dreamt and melodies once heard, it seemed to me that this grand panorama of the Hindu Kush was a different one, for I was driving to the north, towards the storms, the lowlands of Turkistan, the border to Russia, shrouded by creeping clouds of sand, already beset by bitter cold. The journey was harsh; my heart did not rejoice this time as I neared my goal. And the gardens of Tashkurghan, I knew now, were a final oasis, torn from the pitiless desert, sheltered at the foot of the mountains . . .

This desert is fearsome, a dying land. However far north I went, towards the invisible Oxus River and the forbidden Russian border, the signs of death never ceased—skeletons, potsherds and the wind-worn tells of buried cities, fortresses, graveyards. Drought, invasions by nomadic hordes . . . towards evening, in a darkness always suffused with milky light, as from distant stars, I sometimes turned southwards, seeking comfort, and faced the now-familiar blue mountain chain. Its reality was proven, its magical name lived on like a mighty heartbeat. And up above, in the highest still-visible gorges, great fires burned every night. Who warmed themselves there?

One might think that the journey back across the Hindu Kush by the same route would now have been quite an ordinary, indeed a tedious undertaking. Tashkurghan and Haibak, Doab and Doshi . . . But the nights were longer and colder, at four o'clock the stars stood fixed, as though frozen in their blue halos, at six a grey dawn began, seeming in the narrow gorges of Doab to merge with the gloomy day, as though the sun would never shine again; but the blazing splendour of the snowfields at the Shibar Pass was near deadly for mortal hearts and eyes. And over on the southern slope hundreds of men in turbans and fluttering shirts knelt on the river's gravel bank, for it was the end of the month-long fast of Ramadan, a great holiday.

In the grand and changeful panorama of the Hindu Kush I miss the young green, the gentle wind, the stirring song of spring. But we do not dictate our dreams, and I didn't dare look back at the receding snowy peaks as I turned onto the plain. It is not for me to dictate greeting and parting and draw the boundary between reality and vision.

I am left with the magic, the name, the heart miraculously touched.

So far Ella and I had been able to discuss the women of Afghanistan only in theoretical terms. In the weeks we had spent in this devoutly Mohammedan country, we had made friends with farmers and city officials, soldiers, bazaar merchants and provincial governors, we were received hospitably everywhere and began to take to this masculine, jovial, unspoilt people. In the magnificent old city of Herat, we watched youths gather on a lawn outside the gate in the evening to fence and pray together. When we stopped on long shadeless stretches, simple peasants joined us and shared their melons. We never had to pitch our tent and cook our soup ourselves. In the villages, the mayors greeted us, served us tea and grapes. In the evening we were led into beautiful gardens, attentive servants brought out the pilaf, the local rice dish, and while we ate the host paid us a visit with his entourage and often spoke with us at length and in depth.

But we seemed to be in a land without women! We knew the chador, Mohammedan women's all-enveloping drapery, which has little in common with romantic notions of Oriental princesses' wispy veils. It hugs the head, perforated at the face in a sort of grille, then falls to the ground in voluminous folds, barely revealing the embroidered tips and worn-down heels of the slippers. We saw these muffled, formless figures darting shyly down the lanes of the bazaar and knew they were the wives of the proud, free-striding Afghans with their love of company and jovial conversation who spent half the day lounging in the teahouse and at the bazaar. But there was little humanity in these ghostly apparitions. Were they girls, mothers, crones, were they young or old, happy or sad, beautiful or ugly? How did they live, what occupied them, who received their sympathy, their love or their hate? In Turkey and in Iran, we had seen schoolgirls, girl scouts, students, working women and ones active in social causes, already helping to shape the face of their nation, already an integral part of its life. We knew that the young King Amanullah, upon returning from a trip to Europe, had instituted hasty reforms in Afghanistan, attempting to follow Turkey's example in particular. He had moved too quickly. More than anything else he was reproached for emancipating women. For a few weeks the chador had fallen in the capital of Kabul; then the revolution broke out, women returned to the harem, to their strictly cloistered domestic life, and from then on they could not show themselves on the street without a veil.

Were the first stirrings of freedom forgotten, had those few weeks in 1929 vanished from women's memory? Once, when we were the guests of a bright, young, open-minded governor somewhere in the north, Ella ventured the question. Our host had shown great understanding for the imperatives of the Afghan state, speaking of how road construction would open the country to commerce, how industries could then be introduced and schools and hospitals established. Could women be excluded from such a programme of progress? Must they not share in this new life and be liberated from the stupefying constriction of their existence? The governor replied evasively. When we asked politely whether we could see his wife, he agreed, but then found some excuse.

It was not until Qaisar, a small oasis town in the northern province of Turkistan, that to our considerable surprise the Hakim Sahib, the mayor himself, invited us with little ado through a small gate into his home's inner garden, the garden of his wives and daughters. Two young girls in summer dresses, their dark hair shrouded by light, airy veils, approached us smiling. Both were strikingly beautiful—and beautiful, too, was their stately mother with her earnest, friendly gaze. She greeted us under the tall trees, where carpets were laid out and the children played, younger siblings and the daughter-in-law Zara's blond little boy. Her second child slept in a hammock in the shade. The samovar stood off to the side under the projecting roof of the simple clay house; first we were brought a washbasin and towels, then tea and fruits. The pilaf followed an hour later. The mother ate with us at the table in the European manner. The daughters served us and then ate with the children on the carpet, all from the same enormous bowl of rice—and with their fingers. Finally, the servants ate the ample leftovers. While the Hakim's family had the handsome, severe facial features of the Afghans, the servants were clearly of a Mongolian race, perhaps Turkmens or Uzbeks.

After the meal, we were brought silken mattresses and mosquito nets, but we never got around to resting. Though the girls knew hardly a word of French and we had just a few scraps of Persian, we conversed with animation. They brought a light blue piece of silk and a pair of scissors and wanted us to cut them a dress. But we didn't dare try, promising instead to send them French magazines from Kabul with patterns and fashion sections. For the women of Qaisar even Kabul was the wide world, civilization. And yet they'd been taught—at home, of course—to read and write, and knew where India, Moscow, Paris lay; they'd even heard of Switzerland. But they had never taken a journey. They couldn't imagine ever going further than Mazar-i-Sharif, the capital of Afghan Turkistan. Did they even have the desire to explore the world, to lead a different life? Or would they forever remain in the shady garden of Qaisar, surrounded by high clay walls, under the patriarchally strict supervision of their mother and mistress?

The Hakim had us summoned towards evening, when it had cooled off a bit. Little blond Jakub was allowed to accompany us to the car, but the girls remained behind at the garden gate.

No doubt about it, they were bright girls, gifted even, and charming. We remembered their smiles, the alert and friendly expressions on their faces. Only the young daughter-in-law sometimes had a bitter, almost angry look when she took her infant out of the hammock and gave him the breast. Here in her husband's family she was among strangers, after all, with no household of her own, neither freedom nor rights.

When these girls left the garden, they wore the chador—and saw the outside world only through the perforated grille that hid their face from men's curious eyes.

We could hardly imagine such a life. But were these women particularly unhappy? One can desire only what one knows. And was it right, was it necessary to educate them and broaden their minds and give them the goad of discontent? But we soon learned that the question is moot. Today, Afghanistan is developing according to the fateful laws known as progress whose course cannot be checked. And by sending the promised dress patterns from Kabul to Qaisar, we contributed in our own small way towards the consequences of these laws. We fought the chador!

THE WOMEN OF KABUL

I met the woman in the Kabul men's hospital, in the spartan room of the Swiss head nurse, poorly heated by an antiquated electric stove. She had come in a gadi, one of the little two-wheeled hackneys that jauntily trotting horses somehow manage to pull through even the narrowest bazaar lanes of the Afghan capital. She wore the chador, the heavy grey veil that hugs the head like a bonnet and falls in loose folds over the shoulders to the ground—the garment that shrouds the Afghan woman. But she was no Afghan woman; she had grown up on the seacoast of Normandy, a happy child with blonde braids, friends with her brothers, with the yard dog and the heavy-hoofed horses and the languid brindled cows, with the babbling fountain, the cliffs, the beach, the bracing winds of her French homeland. She gave me her hand a bit shyly. Maybe I wasn't nonchalant enough; watching the sad, spectral figure enter, I had felt a crippling sense of horror, almost aversion—and yet it was a long-familiar sight for me. For of course the Afghan women all look the same, in the bazaars, on the dusty streets of the cities and villages, in the walled gardens of private houses. I know only that the Jewish women wear a black chador, the Afghan women grey or light blue, and there may be other differences as well: the upturned shoe tips of the farmwomen, the worn heels of the poor, the rich ladies' embroidered velvet sandals beneath the veil's hem. But one wants to see a face— lively eyes, a pretty mouth, a smile—and all you ever encounter is the little face grille flitting past. And you know that these fearful, helpless creatures can barely see enough through this grille to avoid the swaying camels, the jingling little gadi horses, the men with their cheerful and vigorous stride—they live *in constant fear*.

Having satisfied herself that I was not a boy, the woman awkwardly doffed her chador. Underneath it she was dressed in the European fashion, but not very tastefully and somewhat sloppily. The three of us drank our tea, rather taciturn. And yet I could have asked a hundred questions: Why did you marry an Afghan? Certainly, he's well-born, related to a minister at the royal court, he studied in Paris and already has a high-ranking job in the postal administration. And he's likeable; perhaps you were in love with him then, or you're still fond of him, or of your child, this dark-skinned, unruly, insolent little boy who's so unlike you—did this come as a surprise? What did the lovely name 'Afghanistan' evoke for you, this most foreign place, when, barely twenty, you plunged into a fate unknown—and perhaps for that reason so incredibly alluring—parting far too lightly from all the things you knew? I'd also have liked to learn how things work in an Afghan household where mother and daughters-in-law, sisters-in-law, sisters and poor relatives all live together, feeding from idleness, embroidering a bit and drinking lots of tea, eating sweets, chatting and—that much I'd gathered—not even capable of looking after their children. Faced with the dismal disorder of such a household, the insubordination of lazy maidservants, the spoilt cheekiness of the little boys who soon scorn the women, the filth, the general squalor, the boredom, the women are helpless, not even aware that one can live differently. Was it conceivable that a girl raised in Europe put up with it all, even played along with it, accepted it and sank into the agony of creeping time, each moment lost beyond recall? That she shared this existence day after day, as sharp-tongued as the sisters-in-law and neighbour women, party to the grandmother's tyranny and the endless gossip-mongering, forgetting that outside, just a few steps past the courtyard walls, a bright sky arched over gardens and roofs and streets and fields, over a splendidly self-renewing, comforting, life-giving earth? Had she forgotten all that?

Our hostess, the nurse from Switzerland, did her best to keep the conversation going. She talked about her work: the only European, and the only woman, she supervised fifty male nurses and 120 patients, forced to fight the Ministry of Health for every thermometer, much less alcohol, as alcohol is prohibited in this devoutly Mohammedan country. Every day she herself had to inspect the food, prepared in a clay shed outside the hospital, had to intervene when a lamenting, praying clan gathered around the bed of a feverish relative, had to convince the nurses that beds must be made daily and the desperately ill undressed and washed; she assisted with every operation, gave every injection herself. At home, on Lake Biel, she had two boys being cared for by their grandparents; here, in Kabul, she was earning money for their future. While the nurse talked, as unassumingly as though it were only natural to live a decent life and see things through, duties once shouldered, a whole arduous existence, I observed the taciturn guest.

She ate cake without stopping, dunking the pieces in her teacup; her face, puffy and strangely expressionless, might as well have been hidden behind the veil. 'How is your little boy?' the nurse asked her. And suddenly, silently, she burst into tears. Soon after that her husband came to pick her up. Hastily she donned her chador and left.

I didn't even ask the nurse whether an Afghan woman could get a divorce. It was too obvious that the poor woman would lack the courage now to cast off the chador for good. The languor of her flat, rather pretty face was already oriental, aged or ageless; even when she wept, all that showed was misery, no real sorrow, no regret, no unbroken defiance.

Later I had the opportunity to meet Afghan women— with and without the chador. Most of them were so alike that I can't tell one from the other in my memory. But I also met children; that autumn, last year, the government opened the first girls' school in Kabul and recruited several capable women—the wives of the professors at the French school—as teachers. If you wish to know the state of a people, turn to its youth: here, nothing is disfigured yet, they express themselves in ways unset by convention, undulled by habit, unswayed by external dependencies and existential conditions; here, ability and zest for life manifests itself with lovely unselfconsciousness. The little schoolgirls of Kabul were extremely gifted, lively, receptive creatures, a match for the boys, pretty and with such radiant eyes that it was impossible to imagine these slender little forms and delicate intent faces ever banished to the shadow of the harem walls, the sombre confinement of the chador.

Today in Europe we may have grown sceptical towards the catchphrases of freedom, responsibility, equal rights for all and so forth. But it is enough to have seen at close hand the stifling servitude that makes God's creatures into joy-less, fearful beings—and you'll cast off discouragement like a bad dream and listen to the voice of reason that exhorts us to believe in and fight for the simple goals of a humane existence.

Part Four

THE BANK OF THE OXUS

THE NEIGHBOURING VILLAGE

In the yard, in front of the three domes of unfired clay bricks which house our expedition,[12] Afghan soldiers have pitched their tent. A thin and pathetic tent, dust-yellow like the uniforms and like the desert all around, fluttering in every wind when not sagging in the night rain and collapsing like a slack cowhide. The soldiers, three of them, wear puttees but no socks, and low native shoes with turned-up toes; they don't take a single step without slinging gun and ammunition belt crosswise over their skinny shoulders, and when the sun beats down they take off their helmets and wrap filthy turban-cloths around their heads. They keep a safe distance from our shepherd-dog, who lies chained next to one of the six-wheeled expedition trucks, and they let the villagers feed and tend to them. We pay for what's brought to us: Uzbek bread and grapes, milk, eggs and scrawny hens, and, of course, the firewood. The soldiers do nothing of the kind; they enjoy their steaming bowl of rice every evening and drink tea all the livelong day. That's known as requisition, and they may well think, 'among brothers' or 'me today, you tomorrow', for they are poor devils themselves, Mongols who have little to chew on in their villages up in Hazarajat and may be serving in the military from sheer poverty, in place of someone else who's paying them for it. That doesn't make them any more charitable towards their poor brothers, the Tadzhiks of our village in Turkistan. The Hazara soldiers can't much like the

12 In Kunduz. See note 11.

country, this barren wind-whipped strip of desert on the border of Russia in the far north, nor the job. They watch us suspiciously—what business have we here, we strangers? On desert tracks and potsherd mounds and in heathenish places? Only to make their lives difficult and sour their days, for they must follow us wherever we go, and swallow dust or sit in the icy rain or in the piercing noonday sun when it suddenly breaks through, and like us they must endure the blinding sight of a flat, boundless horizon endlessly flooded with mirroring waves of air . . . Or could I be wrong? Could it be that these shivering lads are neither resentful nor vengeful, nor even curious? That they aren't homesick for their valleys, that every coat fits them, and every bowl of rice goes down well as long as they don't have to pay for it; the great horizon does not perturb them, they don't even see it, at least not with our eyes—and we, we are a matter of indifference to them?

Whatever the case may be, we have nothing to begrudge each other, neither can envy the other an hour spent more easily, we all breathe the same dust, face the same wind— we and the three uniformed men, and the Tadzhiks in their barren fields, their windowless huts, their dead streets. And I walk, walk through these streets, narrow corridors between high, yellow, eroded clay walls; I want to find my way out into the open, to breathe deep, and I don't look around to see whether one of the soldiers is following me as usual. No one is following, there's no one on the streets, but from the roofs, from all sides, I am assailed by the angry barking of the shepherd-dogs, yellow beasts with cropped ears, shaggy fur, wide sets of bared teeth—ready to hurl themselves into the street, at me. I stop, snatch my

coat together, they balk a moment at the threatening gesture, and I walk on. A little square, a tree, the canal, and
children playing with sheep's knucklebones. No reply to
my greeting, and once again walls, breathless constriction,
death-like silence. Then the village comes to an end, the
world opens up, sky and earth are one! Not that the sky is
fair out here, the earth fruitful and blithe. Not that there
are lush pastures, and gentle greenness, a murmuring
brook, a birch grove, and blessed sun, blessed wind—not
that the heart grows lighter. Our village, surrounded by the
desert, is the last semblance of human habitation in a great
place of ruins. And the desert grows, coming from the
north, and wherever I turn I see dying land. Yes, our village
is already gripped by the inexorable destruction like a con-
tagious disease—hence the smell of dust in its streets,
hence the crumbling walls, the empty domes, hence the
feeble fires in the evenings and the moon's ghostly light . . .
And the funereal expressions of its inhabitants, the pale
Tadzhiks, their joyless greetings, their furtive, hasty gait—
what hope should sustain them and their children? Soon
the village will be abandoned, perhaps in twenty years,
perhaps in a hundred. One ruin more, a few rises in the
ground where the domed huts stood, a moon-track, the
dried-up canal, and everything at the mercy of the wind,
smoothed by the wind and constantly covered with
new dust as though by a diligent gardener who tends and
waters his garden, morning and evening . . . And I walk
and I've come out into the open, the horizon is wide and
the afternoon sun plays glittering games, but I am still in
the ruins, on the hard-trodden ground of the sunken city,
and the hill I climb was once its proud citadel. On all sides

deep trenches reach out into the emptiness; these were once the life-giving canals. Gentle barrows spread like the wavelets of the rising flood—once houses, hay-lofts and stalls. Great rectangles stand out, the walls still visible— once caravanserais, filled with the drone of camel bells and with bundles of wares from Antiochia, from Tabriz, Trabzon, and from India, from China! The Silk Road, O roving thought! And I look about, and nothing remains, the bells are buried, the cisterns caved in, the altars cold. In this merciless land, one is tempted to believe the earth is on the verge of extinction, rolling towards its end, even now no hospitable place for the time man is allotted.

I must feel the road underfoot, I tell myself, I must fend off the terrible vision. The struggle with the clouds, with the breath-robbing wind, against cold and weariness, against godless fear, the struggle with the angel and for daily bread, it's all one, and so it was willed for us. What hold can these ruins have over me, or the colour of the unfired clay, of the desert? Just as well reproach the flight of time and wish to turn your back to it, just as well hope to seek refuge from your own failing breath . . .

Now, after all, I seem to have found the way out of the dead city—no more potsherds, no bricks—and can stroll in the former gardens outside it, following the course of a canal. But I can hardly believe my eyes: water runs in the canal, it's alive! It flows through a flat autumn field, the grain can't have been reaped long ago, stray stalks lie among the dry clods of earth, and a little further, at the edge of the field, yellow straw has been piled up in great heaps. Beyond it rise long clay walls, and above them gentle treetops emerge, clothed in coloured leaves—perhaps willows and sycamores, perhaps nut trees? A shady grove, a garden? I walk along the walls, thin grass underfoot, and I hear the barking of dogs and the neighing of horses: a village must be very close, we have a neighbouring village and never knew it, knew only the mounds of potsherds and the nearness of the desert, the seed of death, the fruitless vastness, the terrible unceasing wind . . .

Over with, forgotten—I'm not surprised to see a rider appear now, black hair fluttering beneath his white turban, and I'm not afraid when a few yellow shepherd-dogs shoot towards me a moment later. Already they hesitate, a woman's voice calls them off. Yes, for the first time in ages I hear the voice of a woman, cheerful and imperious, then laughter, and 'biah, biah'—'come here, come closer'. She stands on the edge of the wall, young, all bathed in light, she wears glittering earrings and a voluminous skirt; unveiled, she waves at me, laughing. Below her, behind the wall, as though gathered about her knees, are other women, young and old, and a crowd of children, little boys in embroidered caps, little girls with tightly woven braids; they all cheer and cry 'biah' as if to celebrate and have their fun with me. There I stand, almost confounded, and look at the dogs which crouch and bare their teeth threateningly just a few yards away. But at once the rider arrives, gliding from his horse, which trots alone and wilful into the yard, and the dogs shrink back, growling. The youth in the flowered coat invites me to follow him—the girl, still standing on the wall, inclines her beaming face enticingly— and, before I know it, I am the guest of the village.

The women hang back a bit. The young man leads me across two courtyards to a little terrace of stamped clay where the Hakim Sahib sits on a thick felt rug, mayor and dignitary, handsome and masculine, earnest, amiable. I must slip the overshoes from my Turkmen boots and sit next to him, the children squat in a semicircle, marvelling, the women look at me and exchange whispered remarks.

'Where do you live, who are you?'

We begin our conversation, the Hakim and I, and in the meantime I am fed: a little bowl of a sweet made of sugar and beaten egg white—the youth breaks the flat bread, dips pieces in the white mass, hands them to me, and divides the rest among the children—then green, unsweetened tea; the Hakim personally rinses out the drinking bowl three times. 'Your bread is good,' I say, and they nod: 'We have bread, we have grain and fields, we have sheep, horses, donkeys. We have grapes and melons too. We have a good village, we have water.' And then, at my question: 'We are not Tadzhiks, we are Afghans, and we have come from the mountains.'

They have come from the mountains. Their brothers are nomads, their home is the valleys of the Hindu Kush, or the more distant pastures in the south, which, I don't know. But they have built their huts where the earth is grudging, water precious and life harsh in the great desert winds. And they have kept their good bread and their proud horses, and their women's unveiled appearance. Perhaps they are just as poor as our Tadzhiks, or poorer, for, strictly speaking, there is less water in this village, fewer trees, fewer fields; one can hardly even call it an oasis, and the power of the desert is the same. But what hospitality, what a hymn of praise to existence!

It is evening now, the wind seems gentler, I head for home. And the neighing of the horses from the neighbouring village accompanies me . . .

THE BANK OF THE OXUS[13]

Behind me, in the south, the blue range of the Hindu Kush looms so unreal that only the flooding brightness of the moonlit nights does it justice. Its foot is hidden, talus slopes carry it as though it had no earthly weight. Sometimes, too, it seems to rise from the gardens, one knows not how, from alleys between yellow clay walls, from the little meadows which barely offer room for a few mulberry trees, from the plots of grain and the tiny cotton fields, from the narrow winding bed of a river which must have its source up there, perhaps in a grey waste of scree, perhaps in a beautiful valley. Yes, there are gardens here, seeming to give a little comfort, and behind the crumbling walls live farmers, Tadzhiks, Uzbeks and Turkmens—poor brothers, people like you and me. And when you see a white or a light blue turban, a woman's red veil by day in the fields, or at noon the men who have gathered to pray outside the little mosque, or in the evening, at the entrance to the bazaar, the first warm glow of a samovar, you believe the course of a well-ordered day is assured, a well-ordered life according to laws devised for our protection, for our needs, and you feel almost sheltered.

I made a habit of going to the village bazaar every morning. Soon they knew me, the poor brothers shivering in their quilted tunics, their striped coats, the coppersmiths and the saddlers, the potters, the wool-carders, the grape

13 See note 11.

merchants and the old men who dug out coins for me from
a dented tin, a Hellenistic one, one with a fire altar and a
Kushana king in a pose of adoration, and a Queen Victoria
penny. One stall sold Russian cigarettes and Russian sugar
cubes; many others sold Japanese cloth and Russian head-
shawls, which they tie about their hips as belts in these
parts. And I walked past the butchers' and the grape merchants' stands to the bakers, where round fragrant Uzbek
breads were stacked in swaying towers, and across the
square with the sacks of rice and pepper, where camels jos-
tled, drivers yelled, a shabby soldier kept order and the sun
shone on the righteous and unrighteous hagglers. I
entered the shadows again, the fusty air of the covered
bazaar, filled with strangely drugging smells and the smoke
of small coal fires, found the shoemaker who made me
high Turkmen boots of soft, warm leather, and the tailor
who sewed purple velvet vests on a Singer sewing machine.
Then came the silversmiths' lane; then it suddenly turned
cold, and after the tea and spice merchants with their green
and dust-grey mounds I came out into the open again,
onto a clay bridge, and the sun played with the gurgling
water.

Walking on, I met riders and handsome horses, for
the village belonged to the Afghan province of Turkistan
where the horses are better cared for than the people.

In the afternoon the sun was strong, and in the
evening the sky turned white, and the Hindu Kush shone
in the cold light like a heavenly body. Thus there was
variety in the progression of the hours, and the days passed;
at night I had a fire and slept in the vaulted room of an

old palace. I almost let myself be fooled, comforted by the sight of a little green, and the red glow of a samovar in the dusk, at the edge of the lonely road; almost felt secure in the shelter of the oasis, though it had the smell of the desert wind in its streets and heard the wolves and jackals in the winter nights. But while I maintained the appearance of a well-ordered life, got up, went about my business, grew hungry and ate, grew tired and slept, and watched my brothers live, in their huts, bazaar stalls, places of prayer, or simply walked along the track leading north, into the steppe and the desert, in order to breathe, to move my limbs, to get warm, feel I was alive, defy the hours; as I exchanged Persian words with the Tadzhiks, and laughter, though we did not understand each other, and in fact I was already wordless as though in a too-strong wind which takes your voice away—even as I tried to keep my pride, to be a human among humans, I was no longer fooled: no news reached me, I was far away, the high barrier of the Hindu Kush severed me from the Kabul River, the Khyber Pass and the border of India, the broad swath of desert in the north from the cities of Russia, from Samarkand, Tashkent, Bukhara and the bank of the Amu Darya. And these borders, these barriers, rivers, deserts were impassible for me and my kind! 'The Russian army could be here in a few hours,' I was told by an Afghan official who had heard of the war in Europe and was understandably concerned: Why shouldn't the Russians want to annexe Afghan Turkistan to its Asian lands, harvest a little more cotton? Who would stop them, between the Amu Darya and the Hindu Kush?

So we talked politics a bit, and that same morning I saw the Russian airplane from Tashkent in the blue heights, still hearing the gentle hum of its engine after it had vanished like a blithe silver bird in the clouds over the Hindu Kush. For a long time that was the only sign from the world, the thought of which filled me with unrest and terrible helplessness . . . And I guarded myself against it: how would I have ended otherwise, a prisoner or free?

No, I was no longer fooled by the deceptive sight of a little green, already autumnal now, withered and carried off by the wind, or seduced by the sight of gleaming wings in the blithe sky, a sky I knew could turn fixed and deadly from one hour to the next—a brazen bell with no sound. I was no longer fooled, for out there, very near, a breath's length away from me, was the desert.

The encounter with it was irrevocable. No clock struck there, no laughter rang out, distances could not be measured. A tell suddenly emerged from the desolate plain like an island, I thought it was two hours away from me and of considerable size—but minutes later my foot brushed a few scattered potsherds, and the mound, shrunken, was a meagre accretion of the wind. Yes, and once I thought I saw a stranded airplane ahead of me, some distance away, a metallic gleam in the grey sand, and I approached cautiously, leery of the unexpected encounter. But I walked and walked, and it was—the blue glaze of a potsherd from the Islamic period. Ah, the walks in the desert, aimless, unending, among sand dunes, tamarisk shrubs and the wind-smoothed ruins of old cities, fortresses, cisterns! For one day I left the scant protection of the gardens and went to the north, along the hard track of the donkey-riders and camel-drivers. What did I seek there in the north, what did they seek? But there is another village amid the eroded towers and caved-in caravanserais of a once-flourishing city abandoned by its inhabitants in drought. One last filthy, scant canal remains, cut deep into the hard ground—and it sustains the village. Black-bearded Tadzhiks, their women in red skirts, their children. They live in round clay domes behind walls which are already cracking and crumbling; they own a donkey, a horse, sheep, and in the evenings I see camels come from the desert and turn onto the lane which seems too narrow for their swaying gait. The fields around the village have been wrested from the desert; they must be flooded before even attempting to plough their stone-hard surface. And what could possibly thrive here! Meagre bread, a few melons, a handful of straw. There is no bazaar stall in the village, no baker, no singer, and in the evenings no samovar glows. The Tadjiks live in the desert's proximity as in the face of death and our insignificance—without desire and ambition, plagued only by the heat and drought of the summer, by the icy, dust-choked steppe winds of a long winter, terribly defenceless. I remember how, a few months ago, I first arrived in this land—ancient Baktria, Tokharestan, Turkistan—and thought I would suffocate in the lifeless August nights. How I sighed in relief when I reached the first heights of the Hindu Kush and left the agony of the plain behind me forever! Now I have returned, and the land is wan, and the horror of winter has come. The neighbours in the village bring eggs and chickens, self-baked Uzbek bread, mutton, tomatoes, a load of firewood. It is not hard to build a fireplace beneath a clay dome and stretch a great sheet of canvas before the entrance. If that is not enough to keep out the dust, the driving rain, the violence of the wind—still one can live. Don't they live, my neighbours and poor brothers? And I always wake when the moon grows pale and the yellow dawn of another day spreads, an implacable flood . . .

I set out to the north. Always to the north, driven by a strange perversity; I could just as well walk in a circle, or to the east, or the west, leaving it to chance. Some distance behind a soldier follows, to guard and watch me. Maybe he wonders whether I might not, after all, reach the Russian border by mistake some day. For this desert is no more than thirty kilometres across, and on bright days I seem to see a swath of haze over there, a faint band of smoke, misty clouds of moisture over the river. And to the right a gentle line of hills—perhaps trees, wind-stirred leaves, perhaps black furrowed fields, grazing herds, prosperous farms, perhaps dew-fresh meadows and the sweep of the scythe . . . But these are delusions. I know I will never reach the bank of the Amu Darya, the great Oxus. And in any case no blessed land begins past those banks, here and there is waste and vastness, steppe, desert, hardness and want, endlessness: the heart of Asia. And the banks of the Oxus are gloomy, I'm told—sand banks, wild ducks, a little jungle— it's not worth the trouble.

It's not worth the trouble—

One day I met a hunter. The only weapon he carried was a pole with an iron hook—with that and his three long-eared, silky, swift greyhounds he killed hares, all sorts of birds, sometimes a gazelle. I asked him if he would sell me one of his Tazis. Not for a hundred afghani, said the man, and headed off. I watched him vanish among sand dunes and potsherd mounds, his dogs racing ahead of him like loosed arrows. He must have had a long way home. But what did he care for space, for this day, and the next! What were present and future to him, he who did not fear the sandstorm? Did he know what fortune and misfortune mean, and what our tortured hearts call hope? Now the dust all around was thick as fog, the sky leaden, the pale blue line of the Oxus bank submerged. What was I waiting for? For signs and miracles, stars on the firmament . . .?

It is not the winged impatience of spring, sung by the
poets, open to love, embracing all hopes, kin to happiness.
That season is no more, no more delight, breathing, smiling, striding—it is November, the fury of Asiatic summer
has passed over the land, and the echo of the distant war
does not halt at Afghanistan's mountainous border. The
scanter the news, the rarer and more unreliable the arrival
of the mail from India, the greater the agitation—and if
you're far from the capital, which itself is nothing but an
isolated village, and perhaps a fortress, a feudal residence,
you feel far from the world and foreign to it, cheated of
shared concern and a solemn, selfless stake in the future.
You have dark hours and dark dreams, and you ask yourself: What am I doing, what business do I have here? What
does all this have to do with me?—meaning the donkey-
rider, the soldier, the turban-wearer, meaning the mullah
who stands in front of his little mosque at noon and gives
the call to prayer, meaning the believers who gather, the
farmers, the tea-drinkers and the caravans that pass by
slowly on mountain paths laid down for the past millen-
nium, and the nomads who come down from the high valleys, their summer pastures, towards the south, towards
India. They too follow the laws of millennia, and the laws
of the seasons, the good pastures, as though it had to be, as
though a person had no freedom to choose and were
merely a faithful or unfaithful servant. And the laws are
draconian, the living meagre, the seasons implacable—is

it impossible to escape them? Is there nowhere an open road, a pass leading across to other countries, is it always the same sky, morning and evening, the same cycle, the same call to prayer, and never an answer? And you forget what you're rebelling against, what God you turn to, abject, bitter, perplexed, in helpless distress. You think you're alone. The others, down in the valley, they aren't your brothers. See, they're nomads, they build their yurts, a frame of branches with coarse felt blankets over them and colourful woolen bands for decoration, and their dogs are vicious. See the men there, huddling around a little fire beneath the overhanging cliff; they're hauling slabs of salt from the Pamir to Kabul and Kandahar, they've relieved their donkeys of their burdens and started cooking their rice; they're poor, freezing. See the caravans, swaying camels and singing drivers; they're shadows on the river-bank. And the reddish glimmer high up in a crevice of the Hindu Kush: charcoal burners' fires, I'm told. But is it possible that people spend the icy-clear night there? Are those stars emitting their light, bleak as the milky moon?

The nights are long at this time of year—no need to wait for dawn, it's grey and oppressive, made no mellower by our impatience. But the next day, with the sun already high, my path takes me to Istalif. A pretty name, I think, and past the large market town of Charikar the valley is broad and fertile, one great oasis. After so much desolation in the Hindu Kush and the bitter cold on the Shibar Pass, it's a pleasure to see the red silk turbans of Indian traders, to see the gentle eyes, the pale skin of the townspeople and the brokers from Hindustan after the closed, foreign, slant-eyed Mongol faces tanned by relentless sun and strong wind. The road is wide, lined by poplars. The car rolls purposefully over the soft ground as though smelling the stable. The mountains fall behind, receding to the side.

The town of Istalif lies to the right, bedded in a hollow, rising up in terraces, almost a sea of houses, shadows on the flat roofs, light on the walls, all beautifully rounded and girded by gardens in autumn colour. A sign: 'To Istalif', and I turn off the road, and once again it's a pleasure to drive uphill, between painstakingly watered fields, where farmers at the ploughs drive their black oxen pairs and women in red skirts stoop to bring in the last harvest. Then clay walls, gates, houses, the entrance to the bazaar, covered with boughs. Bowls of brownish grapes, sour milk, heaps of spices; pointed shoes, pottery, whole skinned sheep in the butcher stalls—what a wealthy town! In the chaikhana, the chatting men move together a bit to make space for me on the straw mat and offer me green tea and hard-boiled eggs. After I've eaten and paid a few coins, a boy leads me through the bazaar and up several steep lanes, as if to climb to a vantage point. He wears a purple velvet vest with silver braid, a white shirt, a white turban; he's cheerful and loquacious, pretty as a picture. Then the streets end, and through a little low gate we enter a grove of ancient trees that borders the wilderness; above are the mountains, bare, precipitous slopes, scattered boulders, a milky stream, and not a plant, not a shrub, not a shadow. But under the trees the light is golden, and the stream turns tame. A group of veiled women strolls along the edge of the terrace, where you can gaze out a long way across the gardens, grapevines, flat roofs, over the autumn-vivid valley, follow the white road on the valley floor between its rows of poplars and the blue river that comes down from the north, from snowy ridges bathed in blazing light. The air is fresh, the sky softly hued, almost transparent, the horizon hazy. I feel I've never seen an autumn day like this one! I follow the boy along a footpath that leads out of the grove and across a sunny hillside to the upper part of town.

This is where the potters live. It's early still, three perhaps, and they're at work. Outside, on the roofs of their houses, they've set out their wares to dry: still unglazed and unfired, moist clay, earth shaped by diligent, skilful hands. From the sunny roofs I descend into the courtyards, where the potter's wheels turn, the clay is mixed with water; in a mortar, a boy pounds the blue crystalline mass from which the blue-green glaze is made; next to him, another little fellow crouches next to an aperture from which smoke rises—the kiln. And all around and below me, on all the roofs and terraces, is an array of tea bowls and flat plates, simple lamps and vessels for fruit and sour milk, some smooth, some decorated with engraved patterns, but all blue-green, luminous—for the potters of Istalif know but one colour, one glaze, inventing nothing new, practising their craft as they have learnt it, passing it from father to son and grandson. But just for fun, as it were, as a change and a joy to the eye, they sometimes paint a bowl with rust-brown and yellow spots, daubs and circles, as with a brush dipped haphazard in liquid autumn leaves, they apply a transparent glaze and consign the artwork to the ranks of ordinary wares stacked up in their courtyard next to the baking oven, the firewood, the corncobs, all sorts of winter supplies. They aren't rich, the potters of Istalif—but why should a potter be rich? They have what they need, good clay and water, and the farmers, their neighbours, do their part, with good bread, fat sheep, an abundance of grapes, nuts, sweet almonds and mulberries. And the day is full of cheer and activity, and has its rightness when evening comes and shadows slip over the roofs: Enough! Rest your hands!

I remember then that I'm just a stranger in Istalif, having happened by chance upon this road, their streets, their gardens, their courtyards, tolerated only as a spectator at the threshold of their existence with its peaceful laws. I leave the town and walk without even knowing where, into a long evening and the desolation of the yellow hills that stretch on like a sea. Kill the hours! Curb impatience, stave off the distance! And yet just now I felt at peace with the potters of Istalif, and the earth in the evening light seemed well disposed towards them and me.

Then a man comes out of his garden, greets me, cordial and earnest, and offers me a handful of nuts scooped from his wide belt. He opens the little gate: 'Take them, I have more. Here is my garden, my cottage, the sun still clings in the boughs of the old tree, the fire is already lit on the hearth. Be my guest this evening, step inside . . .'

Sensible people and good friends warn me, advise me against it: Now is not the season, it's cold by night, unsafe by day, snow can fall at any moment, and the road to Ghazni is poor and leads through very lonely mountains. You have time, you're free; wait for a more favourable opportunity to visit the city of the Ghaznavids. There are many things to see there, just think of the tombs: the tomb of the old Sultan Sabuktigin, the tomb of Mahmud-i-Ghaznawi, the tomb of a Sufi poet and that of a holy man. And think of the city wall, more than a mile long, time-ravaged; don't forget to climb up to the citadel, on a round hill in the heart of the city from whose lofty height you command all the streets and see all the valleys, the view is worth it. And then the old bazaar: we advise you as friends, set aside a whole morning to visit this classic and romantic bazaar. There you'll see the handsome, long-haired men of the southern tribes in those brightly embroidered jackets you rarely find these days, merchants of all races, charming lads always ready for a lark; don't forget the saddlers, the coppersmiths, the singers. And the sunset! When do you set out, at four tomorrow morning?

No, I reply, dreamily, rashly, maybe I'll start this very day, but just today—beautiful out, isn't it?—there's so much to do: just today I was asked to go hunting, at two the horses will be saddled and we'll ride up the heights by the Logar. You know I love the cheerful hoofbeats, the supple gallop, I love the hunt on the streambed, on stony slopes, and the final, headlong ride across the broad grassy plain, the race against the shadows. I can't withstand the temptation, you know that. A saddled horse, its mettle, its loyalty, the reined-in joy of living!

Why not? Oh, freedom, freedom! And already I guess the answer: Why not? One day for hunting, one for pleasure, six days of work, and on the next, the seventh, you'll set out on the little trip to Ghazni. And now a few more suggestions . . .

For even if the drive from Kabul takes only four or five hours, in a wild country such trips require careful preparation. You must go to the ministry and ask for permission, if you don't want to freeze miserably you must phone Ghazni (the telephone works) and have them stock wood and light the stove there, and you're advised to take provisions along and bedding. Don't forget the film camera! Toothbrush, towel, warm socks. And fuel! Is the car in reliable working order?

I haven't been to the ministry. I haven't checked the car, bought provisions, looked at the clock. I don't even have cigarettes—and my passport, God knows where my passport is. And this very day I'll drive to Ghazni. What criminal perversity! Do I think of nothing but my horses? And call my blind drifting freedom, a human right . . . ?

But at dawn, waking without cares or oppressive dreams, I remember: it's the day of the hunt in the Logar

Valley, and the day of the trip to Ghazni. The fanfare of
departure—and a beautiful day; the winter sun, heavy as
lead, trickles down the hills, soon to reach the city, wake
the fish in the Kabul River, cover the crenellated roofs in
mourning. It must be around seven—Lord, let it be day!—
the vines in our big garden are yellow, frozen, no longer
touched by dew, no longer gleaming, never again to bear
fruit. Violet, turquoise-green, velvet-grey grapes—and
others, blue as lapis, transparent as glass, milky and sweet
as Original Sin. Too late, too late, and I begin the day—
which could be a special day—like any other: with an
empty heart and an empty morning stomach, guiltless, without purpose and desire. The others remind me, reproach me:
But you wanted both this and that, a bracing ride, and the
start of a not insignificant trip. We were telling you about
Ghazni just yesterday, weren't you listening, have you
already forgotten everything but the tomb of Sultan
Sabuktigin? And the dangers of the journey, the cold?

And the saddlers, I respond, and the fetching lads.
And the singing in the evening . . . no, I've forgotten nothing, faithful servant that I am, I'll see everything and do my
duty, make my report, start on my journey. But let me be,
let me be! It's early yet, I don't know what the hours are
worth and how they pass, I must seize this day—what do
I care for Ghazni, what do I care for a lathered horse, hunting calls, hoofbeats, the mild sun on the slopes of the
Logar? Just yesterday—yes, yesterday—I was there in the
evening with a beautiful, girlish companion: it took my

breath away, I saw peace and beauty all around, my solitary heart wanted to accuse, to plead; I was close to tears. O tenderness, speechlessness, undying desire!

Over already, overcome after all: now, today, it's time to write, to soothe a balking heart. Haven't you seen cities filled with marvels and valleys of austere grace? Are you a weakling, a coward, a wretch and a beggar living from alms—don't you know that Man resembles his God, and only Him, and can snatch from the surging void sounds to touch every heart, and see colours lovelier and subtler than any dream, invent lineaments of grace, erect altars of light and fire; that he can live without hope, be brave and wrest his prayer from the dreadful abyss of his solitude?

There I found myself, in the shaded middle of a glorious day, alone, bent over my work. 'You shall work for six days,' I wrote conscientiously, made no more accusations, no more demands, was without forethought. What am I writing of, so eager and assiduous? Of the cities and towns of Afghanistan, its peculiarities, its good and evil spirits? Of Herat the Splendid and its towering minarets, of Balkh, for its historic name, of Mazar-i-Sharif's white flocks of doves? Oh, stop asking these questions, keep your knowledge to yourselves, the names, the suggestions, and leave me in peace to be blind and deaf, writing to the very last hour. I haven't been to Ghazni yet and I'll set out today for certain. Wait for another season? And wait till mourning ebbs like an evil element and joy commences like the clatter of hooves and the sound of fanfares? I've demanded no comfort, awaited no special hour; evening's wondrous splendour will accompany me: It's time! We're setting out on the trip to Ghazni!

Part Five

TWO WOMEN ALONE IN AFGHANISTAN

TWO WOMEN ALONE
IN AFGHANISTAN

Two women travelling alone! 'How did you manage to get around? How did you find food, where did you sleep? Didn't you have any bad experiences?'

Now that we've crossed the famous Khyber Pass[14] and reached India's sheltered English settlements, we're asked the same questions over and over again. And when we reply truthfully: 'With our Afghan friends, we felt safe as in Abraham's bosom,' we're met with an Englishman's sceptical smile, or the admiration, tinged with indulgence, of those who have never travelled without an elaborate cold lunch in the 'tiffin box', a dozen bottles of iced beer and, alongside the chauffeur, a houseboy to prepare the bath and iron the dress shirt in the evening. The British, you see, are the most conservative nation on earth, and they can't forget that, a hundred years ago, Afghanistan's wild mountain tribes inflicted several defeats upon the English troops that had marched in from India, attacking the utterly demoralized expeditionary army on its desperate retreat to the Khyber Pass and massacring it so brutally that the incident still ranks as one of the British Empire's greatest catastrophes. What's more, between the English-governed northwestern border province and sovereign Afghan territory lies the swath of no man's land known as

14 As Schwarzenbach and Maillart did not cross into India together (see 'Onward to Peshawar . . .'), Schwarzenbach seems to be taking poetic licence here.

the Tribal Territory, where the warlike and passionately democratic Mohmand, Shinwari and Waziri tribesmen are subject to no law but their own. And though they also guarantee the safety of the Khyber Road—from sunrise to sunset no shot is to be fired there and all are to travel in safety—in the view of the English authorities no lady may cross the pass unaccompanied by a gentleman. For beyond the Tribal Territory lies Afghanistan, homeland of the same unruly and warlike tribes, or their close kin. What more natural assumption for an Englishman than that this mysterious, wild land is uncivilized and dangerous, at least in the British sense of the word?

And yet we'd travelled there, two women alone, without a houseboy and chauffeur, without even a gentleman. We possessed no iced beer, no firearms, we barely understood a few scraps of Persian. We'd gone without an interpreter as well. Not once were we asked to show our passports or papers for our Ford with the Grisons licence plate. No one tallied our foreign currency, or forced us to pay a fee for the radio (which had long ceased working anyway). Only in one little corner, lost to the world, were we asked if we were Japanese, but really, no harm was meant.[15]

We had just one unpleasant incident in the Hindu Kush, in a nomad camp 2,500 metres above sea level. As Ella Maillart and I distributed balms for inflamed eyes and chapped hands, quinine pills for fever and licorice for coughs and the evil eye, as the women folded back their

---

15 Oddly, the positive-minded Maillart is much franker about a number of (minor) 'unpleasant incidents' of official harassment, tensions, etc. which Schwarzenbach downplays or ignores.

black veils, smiling shyly, and brought us babies afflicted by various maladies, some joker stole one of our Leicas from the automobile the tribal elder had ordered him to guard. The act ran counter to the laws of hospitality and all our experiences. We were at quite a loss for what measures to take. Should we immediately threaten them with the police? Hardly—the organs of the central government are not exactly beloved of the nomads; at most we would have made ourselves unpopular and the Leica would promptly have vanished forever. So we decided to complain bitterly to the malik, the aged chieftain of the nomad tents: 'We are your guests and gave your women medicine, and under your men's protection we were robbed. Is that your hospitality?' The white-beard looked troubled as well, and he clearly knew his flock: one of the young men hurried off and brought the camera back a few minutes later. He explained that his little son had stolen it, the good-for-nothing rascal. The tribal elder berated the culprit in a resounding voice, spat forcefully several times and then invited us to a conciliatory evening pilaf. The embarrassing incident was quickly forgotten and, incidentally, did not repeat itself. The Afghan nomads, regardless of their tribal affiliation, were once more or less warlike, but they are unspoilt, quick to jest, helpful and hospitable. This much is certain: they wouldn't have let a hair on our heads be harmed.

But Afghanistan has more than just nomads. It has city dwellers and villagers, landowners, sedentary farmers, priests, mayors and the civil servants of a modern state in the building. In all the larger cities and along key stretches of the well-travelled roads, the Postal Ministry has set up state hotels offering rooms and beds, a washroom, a kitchen at fixed prices. You can always get tea there and usually pilaf as well, the national rice dish. Some romantics and sincere friends of an old Afghanistan uncorrupted and untouched by novelty deplore the establishment of these state hotels. Undeniably they place some restrictions on personal freedom, for as a traveller you are simply forced to stay in these rest houses and order your tea there rather than drinking it with your brothers in a chaikhana by the roadside or at the bazaar. But progress—in many ways a questionable force, and certainly often abused—follows fateful laws. The sincere aficionado of Afghanistan will welcome the fact that hospitals and schools are being established. He regards it as an urgent necessity that roads be built and the land opened to commerce. He knows the aim is to eliminate poverty and encourage the exploitation of natural resources. He understands that this must be done by rationalizing cotton production, for instance, or by inspecting the karakul (Persian lamb) hides. He does not object to building factories and workers' settlements in place of nomads' camps. He even welcomes women's emancipation, still barely begun and little in evidence. But only with pain and regret does he acquiesce in the overturning of the beloved old traditions and conditions, in 'purchasing' safe and genuinely navigable roads with state hotels rather than staying with nomads and village mayors. There is a tragic element in the problem of progress that one now sees at work in Afghanistan. You feel just a faint stirring of hope, and doubt, that in this independent land between India and the Asian republics of the Soviet

Union it might after all be possible, contradicting all the laws of development, to combine the old virtues of the Afghans with those inevitable innovations which, despite their evils, still give the West the persistent appearance of supremacy.

Be that as it may, on our journey we followed our conscience and favoured romanticism. From Herat we could have taken the usual route to Kabul via Kandahar and Ghazni; then we would have encountered trucks everywhere along the desolate, hot stretches through the desert, we could have bought gasoline and at the end of almost every leg we would have found a hotel. At most, the fact that the bridge over the Helmand had been washed away by spring rains and not yet repaired would have marred this convenient solution. But we were lured by the 'Northern Road', though the only European in Herat had given us quite an alarming picture of it. He was a young Pole, a specialist for road construction who had to know what he was talking about: never could a Ford, however powerful, surmount thirty per cent grades on mule tracks, cross rivers and defy sand dunes. We risked it nonetheless. The aim was to cross the mountains north of Herat and reach the valley of the Murghab, and then—always hugging the Amu Darya and the border of Soviet Russia—drive across the province of Afghan Turkistan to its capital, Mazar-i-Sharif. There the road would take us southwards across the Hindu Kush through the Shibar Pass and all the way to Kabul. Yet the young Pole was right, as were the Afghan authorities, who had blocked the 'Northern Road' for trucks from Herat to Maymana. For one thing, the old bridge over the Murghab had been washed away. A new bridge, thirty miles downriver, had apparently been completed, but that stretch of road existed only on the map. There was much sand and many steep ramps for which our Ford—and no doubt any other car—would have been no match.

And in those August days in Turkistan the heat was so great that we could drive only in the evening or the early morning hours. The car seethed and swallowed the fine, sticky, pore-clogging loess, which is known as a highly fertile soil but which gives the land a hellishly monotonous look.

If we made our way through all of Turkistan despite all these tribulations and without the slightest accident, if our memory of the mountain paths and semideserts of ancient Bactria is a tranquil one, filled to the brim with a wealth of life, we owe it to Afghan hospitality. We stopped worrying where we would find something to eat, where we would spend the midday hours and what the next night would bring.

In the first village past Herat, in the mountains, the mayor received us with a large entourage and regaled us in a cool room in the heart of his fortress-like house. The grapes he had fetched for us from his garden were sweet, tender-skinned and still warm from the sun. That evening we reached Qal`eh-ye Now and soldiers led us through the small bazaar to the governor's residence. In a flower garden enclosed by high clay walls we were shown to a new guesthouse, clearly never before occupied, first brought tea and then a chased bowl with a beautifully curved, beak-spouted jug, skilfully wielded by the servant as we washed our hands. After that the young servant sat in the garden, waiting, discreetly observing every move we made, divining our wishes—when a gate opened in the wall and a small torch-lit procession approached: white-turbaned attendants bearing the pilaf, a rice dish with chicken and stewed and roasted mutton. Bowls of vegetables came with it, little plates of piquant spices and quince jam and round, flat breads, grapes, melons, peaches, a groaning board of the loveliest fruits. The governor, our host, visited us late in the evening after the meal. The next day he accompanied us in his car down new mountain valleys to his residence amid an old garden in Bala Murghab.

On the way we experienced a festive reception in the village of Darreh-ye-Bum. We were led on horseback from the road to the tent which had been pitched for us. The governor ate with the men, and servants brought us a bowl filled with mast and doogh, a kind of yogurt, here sour milk, thinned with water and seasoned with herbs. A sheep, slaughtered in the governor's honour, was stewed and roasted and consumed to the last morsel; we were served a few fat pieces on a skewer with our rice. In Bala Murghab, there was fish from the river which peters out into the sand somewhere near Merv but here was still a fresh, deep mountain torrent. We spent two days in the ancient residence where courtyard followed courtyard, with numerous servants and armed guards in the gateways. We slept on the tamped clay roof and gazed out over the garden's rows of poplars at the yellow plain that flickered in the heat, where the great steppes of Asia began.

I remember a morning reception given by the Hakim of Qaleh-ye Vali. They served, as everywhere, red tea and green tea. Connoisseurs opened the melons and tasted them before we were offered the dexterously carved slices. Through a little window in a carved wood frame we looked out from our dark, cool chamber in the seraglio at the village bazaar, where nomads on horseback and on foot, camel drivers and farmers with their donkeys had gathered for the market day. In Qaisar, we spent the hot hours of the day with the mayor's friendly, dignified wife and lovely daughters in the garden, where carpets were spread out in the shade of a tree and the table was set in the European manner. The rice was served to us at the table. Only the mother joined us at our meal; meanwhile, the daughters and grandchildren ate their pilaf on the carpet, skilfully fishing out not just the rice with their fingers but also the scarce meatballs and the vegetables swimming in fat. Off to the side, next to the samovar, the servant women, slant-eyed Uzbeks in wide, colourful trousers, tucked into the remaining mound of rice. Then we slept on silken mattresses under gossamer veils until it grew cooler outside.

And finally I remember the rich man from Shibargan. One evening—it must have been around nine—we'd reached the bazaar, lit by many coloured lights, and asked a policeman whether we could spend the night there. In exultant affirmation he jumped up onto our running board and led us to a great courtyard and into a garden that lay beyond it. In the middle of the garden, the clay terrace was lit by petroleum lamps and spread with carpets. We were received there by the owner, a friendly man with a narrow

face and a shrewd, pleasant gaze, as though he had
expected us. We took off our shoes, and servants brought
us cushions, tea, and a basin to wash our hands. In no time
a sumptuous pilaf was served. The moon rose as we ate;
the garden was transformed into an image from a fairy tale.
Though unfortunately able to exchange but a few words
with our host, we spent the entire next day in Shibargan,
seeing the rich man's gardeners, servants, friends and
housemates. Before parting, we ate with him one last festive rice dish.

Recently, a Swiss man asked me whether the natives'
food was even edible and whether I hadn't been afraid to
sleep in these people's midst without any protection. The
good man really had no idea of Afghan hospitality!
Despite the various mentions here of rich, spicy pilaf
meals, it must be said that by far not all the inhabitants are
able to afford rice and mutton. In the nomads' tents, there
is often nothing but sour milk and a little bread. And in
many villages the poor people don't even have that. In
Turkistan, where the gardens and bazaar stalls brim with
fruits in the summer, a few months later I saw the relentless winter loom. Then the same landscape was reduced to
a wasteland scourged by the icy wind and cloaked in dense
swaths of dust, and life in the farmers' clay huts was quite
spartan. But despite these worries, it was at this very time
that laughing, waving women met me in the last village on
the desert's edge. They took me to the Hakim, who sat on
a felt carpet, smoking a hookah. While I was offered bread
and a bowl of unsweetened tea, young and old surrounded
me, the children goggled at me, the pretty girls felt my

clothes, the doctor asked me friendly, earnest questions and gave me a horse and a guide so that I would find my way home. True warmth in the desert village and in the opulent garden of Shibargan—this virtue makes the Afghans dear to me.

In one of the lovely, sprawling gardens of the Persian city of Isfahan, at the end of a long pool that cuts through the rose beds like a waterway, lies a small palace they call 'Chehel Sotun'. The name means 'forty pillars'. And indeed the graceful, airy building consists of nothing but a grove of slender wooden pillars that strain up vainly like saplings trying to grow into the sky, supporting a flat, weightless roof; the back wall, colourfully decorated with marvellously delicate mosaic tendrils, fantastic flowers and stars, is barely visible in the muted cool of the columned hall. If you count carefully, though, there are only twenty pillars—and if you wonder then at the name 'Chehel Sotun', you need only follow the gardener to the far end of the waterway to see, at an other-worldly distance, the twenty pillars and their symmetrical, unbroken reflection.

But the number forty has yet another significance. I was still ignorant of it, and knew Afghanistan only by name, when an Afghan friend told me that in his home-land there were forty kinds of grapes.

'Why forty?'

'Forty,' he said, 'means countless, infinite quantities, it means sweetness, infinite extravagance!'

Overcome by memory and homesickness, he spoke of nothing but the bewitching forty-fold profusion of the grapes of Herat and Kandahar. But though I listened to him and these words about the forty kinds of grapes lingered in my mind, tied to the vision of a promised land, at the time I did not even desire to set foot there. You cannot love what you have not embraced and seen with your own eyes; longing itself is never anything but loneliness surging and bleeding away.

At the time, as it happened, I was about to leave Persia, driven by the notion that somewhere there must be milder and more familiar-seeming regions, why perhaps a childhood shore, the promised earth. I did not feel equal to the Asiatic wasteland—though as yet I had no conception of its full scale, its terrors, its heartrending play of colours and its crushing, brazen power! In fact, I was merely travel-weary and wanted to go home. I feared I'd gone a step too far and, albeit unintentionally, crossed the boundary of the sphere human beings are allotted. Yes, I feared punishment! As though it weren't true that our heart can bear everything, and everything and nothing can break it, as though sin and repentance existed—and not those rare moments, the unexpected, merciful encounters.

What does it help me now to think back on the reeling despair that seized me and declare it a mistake! Should I have set out in high spirits with a spring in my step? I did not. Should I have had more faith in the earth's friendly forces and felt certain and invulnerable at the wounding sight of flame-hued horizons? I could not do it, I was terribly vulnerable. Should I have justified myself, raising my eyes to the mountains? Oh, I tried, and always in vain . . .

And so one day I wanted to break away, not knowing exactly from which fate, seeming to grasp only that I had been struck by calamity, as anyone can be, and now must stand apart, silent. How do the others live, I asked myself, how do they bear this land and the day to come, how do they bear it? But should the dusk of rapture fall once more, this shadowless day ebb, the deer stand on the sloping winter meadow already cloaked in fog; should I be granted one more such innocent hour, I will lower my eyes and repent, and never again lead myself into temptation, but admit: we are at home in but a narrow precinct, can cover but a tiny distance—and beyond, at an immeasurable distance, the ships land on death's shores.

Let them tell me of Afghanistan's forty kinds of grapes and seven wonders, the looming towers of the Musallah outside Herat's city walls—of Samarkand, the Golden Gate! Succumb to the old enchantments, ill-fated longings? To foreignness, sky-wide, world-encompassing? God preserve me! That was no prayer, I had no wishes, and I'd already written everything down, forgotten it. Not a word too much . . .

I told myself I'd never return to Asia—let Afghanistan remain a name, the Hindu Kush and Turkistan visions shrouded in sound and smoke, paradises the happy, untrodden valleys. It seemed just as clear to me that I would never pick up a pen again, fill a page with writing. The profession seemed too onerous, a perpetual mirror of our unredeemed existence, which I was also so loath to accept and endure. Over and over again to meet the morning hour anew, the day, the ever-estranged world, to touch them and wring one word from your stricken heart—and know: this will not last, this is the moment of parting, already forgotten. But, still exhausted and blinded by pain, you must set off again, and who will make it worth your while? Is it worth the effort?

But I have forgotten how to ask such questions. Whereas the sound of Chehel Sotun has lingered in my memory, the image of its columns, rising towards the bright Persian sky, and their counterparts, immersed in blue depths. And in Herat I tasted forty and more sweet and tart, many coloured and tender-skinned grapes, down to the golden spheres they call there the grapes of the king, and I spent stifling-hot August nights in the shadow of the gigantic minaret clad in brilliant colours. Even the north wind, never-ending, surging like a sea, brought no relief, but only burning sand from Turkistan's deserts.

I learned little that was new, but I saw everything, experienced everything first-hand—and even in the outermost desolation of the Lataband all I felt was the rigid pain of parting.

Part Six

ONWARD TO PESHAWAR...

For months in Afghanistan I'd dreamt of this day, the day of departure, and imagined this journey, the drive to the Khyber Pass, into India's wild frontier range—and then, far below, at the end of countless serpentines, the view of the plain, the Land of Five Rivers.

Over, the hardship and danger, the too-long, too-lonely road, the too-harsh climate; forgotten, the steppes of Turkistan, beset by howling winds, and their oases, besieged by yellow sandstorms; overcome, the vast desolation of the Hindu Kush, the biting cold on the Shibar Pass, the sight of bleak charcoal burners' fires, black nomad tents, mud-brick villages huddled in the early light—and that endless-seeming night in the gorge of Doab! The sky was nothing but a narrow, blue, steel-hard band between darkly looming cliffs; beside the sloping path, barely two steps across, flowed the dark water of the Kunduz. Forgotten, overcome!

The new day broke cold and sober, a December day like many; snow lay on the Paghman hills that rose airy at the edge of the golden Kabul plain, auguring greater heights, a sea of mountain chains and valleys. Now the time had come. And so, at an hour long predetermined, I took my leave and asked myself in vain: How was this determined, what is the point of this decision, this fiction of our freedom, tasted with bitterness? And owned at the last moment: I didn't foresee this hour!

But it was too late. The winter is harsh in Afghanistan.
A few more weeks or days, and snowfalls would have
blocked the Lataband, avalanches would have severed
the road to India. And I would have had to wait, idle,
unwilling—then what? There was talk in Kabul of the
Russians who might march into Turkistan, advance across
the Hindu Kush, threaten India. There was talk of a gasoline shortage; hadn't it happened recently that none of the
capital's three gas stations had even a few gallons to offer?
The whiskey from Peshawar, from Mister Gai's shop, had
become more expensive; there was talk of that, huddled
around the fire, and the difficulty of obtaining wood in
the capital of this deforested mountain land—already
the schools were without heat! In the only hotel, a few un-
employed Czechs without passports waited for permission
to travel to France via India and join the Legion they'd
heard rumours of. An earthquake gave us a fright. In the
middle of the night, the door of my room flew open; outside, a weird wind swept over the frost-stiff bushes in the
garden; it came neither from north nor south but seemed to
drop from the sky and then fell silent. All kinds of clouds
massed on intangible horizons; we huddled by the radio and
heard of burning villages, battalions freezing to death in
Finland. We were far away; the Khyber Pass was still open,
and, as they did each autumn, endless caravans of camels,
entire nomadic peoples with their tents and household pos-
sessions trekked from the high pastures in the Hindu Kush
down to their winter quarters across the Indian border. One
bright morning in the north, in a flawless sky, we saw the
silver wings of the Russian airplane that sometimes risked
the flight from Tashkent to Kabul. On lathered horses we

rode through the shimmering brown Logar Valley and back home along the velvety valley floor. And so, time and again, evening came. I had a few modest wishes: that Mister Gai would send me a new typewriter ribbon from Peshawar, that the little shop next to the Kabul Bridge, at the entrance to the bazaar, wouldn't run out of American cigarettes. That a good friend would lend me his good, swift horse for the next hunt, that the ground beneath the hoofs would be soft, the sun would be gracious and shine.

Time and again it shone, and in the early, still-anxious hours transformed the grim gloaming into the radiant start of new days! It is not necessary to hope in order to take action; it is not necessary to succeed in order to endure!

This is how we lived in Kabul. It was a modest colony of Europeans, small in number; they baptized their children, and were just preparing to celebrate Christmas when I had to set out. I was advised to stop at the beautiful Moghul gardens of Nimla and spend the night in Jalalabad. Jalalabad? I recall having heard the name months or years before; a road was supposed to branch off there towards sacred, forbidden Kafiristan. But now, at this time of the year, its villages were buried beneath deep snow, and the road might be nothing but a mule track. After that, I was told, you drive across a wide plain superbly framed by white ranges, overtaking mass migrations of nomads heading south, and reach Dakka, the Afghan border post, forsaken amid barren hills. By noon you've already reached the Khyber Pass!

All was as described—but my friends in Kabul had forgotten to speak of the Lataband, a major pass that is higher and more difficult, more dangerous, more dramatic than the famous Khyber Pass. I will never forget it. Perhaps it is only the unhealing wound of parting, that hour so hard to describe, empty, as it were, devoted to nothing but blind, deaf courage; perhaps it is that last moment, irrevocable, already past, when the friendly old man in the turban pushed open the gate and I told myself: You must keep a firm grip on the steering wheel—on Kabul's main road, the clay is sodden, a foot deep—you must get your hands on some gasoline, find the way, you must, *must* . . . and found myself on the route of Alexander's army, without shedding a tear or taking a backward glance. The Lataband was a mountain wasteland, plunged in dead light, with a host of caravans. Is it useful to travel this road, mile by mile, and go on living this way, irrevocably?

The groves of the Moghul gardeners in Nimla, bathed in moonlight. Then wasteland again, ever-vain, ever-renewed courage. At the Khyber Pass, English customs officers asked for my papers. 'When was the last time you crossed this border?' I had great trouble explaining to them that I had never crossed this border, had never seen them before. Whence comest thou, stranger?

They were bemused. Via Persia, Turkistan . . . Why certainly, all the roads are open, and lead nowhere, nowhere.

That same day I saw India. The car flew along on the asphalt Khyber Road, watchtowers, railroad tracks, the walls of Fort Jamrud, the railroad station of Landi Kotal, curves, signals, my breath caught. And I cried out to myself: You yourself made the decision, you yourself are at the wheel! But those were words, words.

There, at the end of the serpentines, lay India. In the immeasurable plain, Indus and Kabul converged, praying men knelt by the shoulder of the road. Stop, take a look—where is the Promised Land? Sorrow, unparalleled emotion—and I remember the pinnacles of the Hindu Kush, bathed in brazen light. I will never see them again.

I'd grown used to counting each kilometre and gaining ground foot by foot, from the Simplon Pass and the plains of Italy, the hills of Yugoslavia, the banks of the Danube and the Bulgarian rose fields to the radiant gates, towers and people of Istanbul; from the Black Sea and the lush shore of Trebizond to the foot of Mount Ararat, jutting solitary into Anatolia's clouds; from the cliff town of Maku to the blue mountains of Tabriz and the eternal, snow-streaked peak of Mount Damavand; from the hot, fever-hazed basin of the Caspian to the lonely Mongol tomb on the edge of the Turkmen Steppe—and on and on, to the golden dome of the sacred city of Mashhad, to the desert border of Persia and Afghanistan, to the immortal minarets of the Musallah outside Herat, to the Murghab, petering out into the sand near Merv, to the Oxus bank and the lonely, wind-scourged sweeps of Turkistan, to the gorges and the magnificent Hindu Kush passes, to Kabul and Ghazni, to the Khyber, the gate to India—and thousands of miles through lands bathed in moonlight, the cities of Hindustan, glimmering with carpets, pools, flower gardens and white marble, all the way to Bombay. There was the sea and the end of my journey, and swimming in the warm salt water of the gently curving bay of Bandra I saw a horizon of palms, straw huts, white cattle, and heard the sirens of ships returning home.

The Indian Ocean, the Arabian Sea—everything is different now, utterly different, patience is exhausted, the will crippled as in a dream, and the moon has set, the steamship churns its way westwards. I need only wait, like the other travellers, and one day I will land in Genoa. Little is asked of us, only this: to set our watches back a half or full hour each day, for we are sailing around the globe, racing the sun!

Aden, Mocha, Massawa, the Red Sea, the Suez Canal, Port Said—mere stations along the way, mere names, meaningless, fleeting. For our homecoming, it matters not whether the sea seems endless to the gaze, ruffled by sunlight and breezes, or whether shores appear, deserts are mirrored, cliffs mass on the edge of Arabia Felix. How many miles, how many days, how many paper flags on the—for all I care—imaginary map? But it's hot, the air like lead, sleep is heavy—and the hours slip over the deck, over me, without real substance.

I count on my fingers: four days since Bombay. And I hear someone say, leaning on the railing next to me and gazing at the night-black sea: 'Tomorrow we'll be in Aden. A depressing little town! Nothing to see, not a patch of greenery, no temples, no monuments, not a decent restaurant to be found, the bar in the Crescent Hotel is a joke, the prices are outrageous, the climate's dreadful. It's not worth going ashore!'

And his neighbour, a ship's officer, announces: 'They won't let the passengers go ashore anyway. How long will we stay? No one knows, perhaps two hours, perhaps two days. Yes indeed, that happens, it depends on the British harbour authorities. There's a war on, sir, a war—and we are a neutral, Italian company and offer no guarantee that the journey will proceed without disruptions . . .'

In a dream, a bit later, I remember a class in school: '*Aden*, children, on the Persian Gulf, on the Gulf of Oman, on the Panama Canal? What a muddle, for shame! Why, Aden—remember that now, and write it down fifty times as a punishment—lies in the southwestern corner of Arabia, at the mouth of the Red Sea, not the Dead Sea, between Asia and Africa, a stronghold of great importance to the British World Empire.'

And I dreamt of the Queen of Sheba and desperately cast about for the lovely name Hadhramaut, where skyscrapers were invented in the midst of the sandy desert. Dreams, dreams, of course, and nothing more! When I woke, it was to the obligatory pageant, morning fog, a little yellow on the horizon of the sea the poets praised—and a new day's sorrowful rebirth.

Then I saw cliffs, and the engine's churning ceased. The sun must have risen—the ship's unreliable clocks, constantly leaping about, showed eight—but the sky was grey, the sulphurous glow hid behind a dense drove of clouds and the cliffs seemed risen from a terrible void, brazen, black—no happy coast, this first glimpse of Arabia!

Great excitement on board our steamship; the German passengers had their passports taken away, Englishmen patrolled in khaki shorts and pith helmets, the Italians brandished papers importantly and refused to give any   information. And what about going ashore? At your own risk! And leave the camera in your cabin, if you please! The departure for Massawa, the Ethiopian port of the future, will take place punctually, we don't know exactly when. Yes indeed, young Signore, no question about it, what you see before you is Aden . . .

And I found myself on land, in Aden, no question about it. The black cliffs formed an arena, bare, treeless, without springs, and seemed to cast no shadows. Bedded in their cruel lap lay this human settlement: Aden. Every three, every ten years rain falls and fills the gigantic tanks that hold several million litres and were wrested from the rock in prehistoric times. Used to this day by the black coolies, they descend from the heights of the cliffs to the sea, cascading cisterns dammed in a ravine. Eight annas, please, to enter the gardens and view our tanks! The gardens! A bit of greenery, morning-fresh, bedded like emerald in the wasteland where we live with our bazaar lanes, barracks, shanties; an English, an Arab and a very large Jewish cemetery; hospitals, schools, police offices, a radio station, a hotel, a cafe. Seven young, blond Englishmen are just having their breakfast there, and next door rupees are changed into pounds and pounds into lira at the best of rates, and Japanese kimonos and American cigarettes are sold for throwaway prices. An asphalt road leads up from the harbour where triangular sails swell on the masts of broad seagoing barges—steered by black, narrow-eyed, narrow-hipped lads with the gift of wondrously mirthful sinners' laughter. Over there, where white pyramids gleam, the beach is flat, the heat incredible: these are the salt pans exploited by the Italians.

But two crags close in, forming a pass and a gate—fortress walls run down from the heights and arch to form a bridge over the road, the sea is left behind, the arena closes—and the sea of roofs at my feet is the old, true Aden, the city of Hindus, Arabs, half-breeds and Negro boys, a filthy, wretched place, an ancient one laden with secrets, rich in ivory and sandalwood, shimmering with alabaster in bright nights. My well-meaning guide shows me the new cinema and the prison, its yellow walls spiked with broken glass, the barbed-wire fences around the barracks of the penal battalions, the cannons on the brows of the cliffs—thousands of them, this fortress is impregnable—the little girls' schools and the English church, and bestows upon me, charging one and a half rupees or two shillings for the wait, a bright red flower from the—God knows!—miraculously watered garden of nameless Arab kings.

It was by chance that I saw the face of Sheba hewn in alabaster and her name set in wonderfully ingenious-looking pictographs on the moon-coloured stele. For I found a museum belonging to a Jew: a basement room. It cost six annas to have the rusty lock opened. There coins were arrayed, shattered feet, coats of mail, there hundreds of alabaster faces gazed down at me, long-nosed and all alike, bearded ancestors, kings, gods, priests, and next to them their bloodthirsty, placid, expressionless moon- and mother-goddesses. It took my breath away; I was glad to reemerge into the salty sea air. A whiskey! An Arabian coffee, a French or pseudo-English pastry, a Camel cigarette!

And all was to be had. The young Englishmen, pith helmets tucked under their arms, ordered steak and French fries. The sun of Aden at last broke forth from powerlessly dissolving clouds.

I don't remember exactly how I reached the sea again and the boarding stairs. The engines churned and thumped, I set my watch and saw that it was evening.

Aden, I told myself, Aden, that was Aden, I hammered it into my head. And through the porthole I saw the vision of a cliff arena bathed in the undying cosmic light that would return in the morning, and a dark-skinned boy bracing his bare feet against the wall of his heavy, ancient rowboat, without a parting gesture.

There is little to report about this trip. It's the usual home-
ward route for ships from India, taking about thirteen days
from Bombay to Genoa and stopping in Aden and Port
Said, perhaps in Massawa, an Italian port in Eritrea. We
sailed through the Arabian Sea, the Red Sea, the Suez
Canal and the Mediterranean. In Port Said, the weather
would suddenly turn; a real, European winter set in. Until
then it had been hot, you felt India's tropical humidity,
then the burning breath of Arabia's deserts.

In Massawa, the climate had to be African; even now,
in January, the Italians wore pith helmets and white uniforms. The sun broke forth from evening clouds, its rays
fell like rain, drumming on the harbour's corrugated iron
roofs. The entire, ugly city consisted of warehouses, customs and other official buildings, export businesses and
pseudo-Italian cafeterias. You drank Italian liquors, paid
with Italian money and read here and there, on the signs
of shipping companies, the name Addis Ababa. Behind the
city, yellow treeless hills began. In a lagoon floated an island
covered with dense, tall green thickets.

Under the awning of a little bar on the wharf I drank
an authentic and very strong coffee alongside dock
workers and a young sailor. Negro boys squatted on the
dock, guarding the heavy hawsers of our white steamship
'Biancamano'. Hearing the steam siren, I went back on
board. All the stewards and sailors who had been given

leave returned from town with little sacks of coffee they'd bought for their families back home in Italy. The band played the Giovinezza[16] and military marches. In the dark, the sea looked smooth and silky, little fishing boats with triangular sails glided past us like birds: that is all I saw of Eritrea.

The Arabian coast had been out of sight ever since Aden. And in Aden, Arabia had been a rocky amphitheater, a volcanic landscape without vegetation, with fortresses on every ridge, barbed wire, barracks—and the white mountains of the salt works on the flat beach past the harbour. I'd had a very different image of Arabia: desert sand, the gleam of ivory, camels' watering holes, the buried cities of the Queen of Sheba . . .

It took us four days to cross the Red Sea. I've never seen so dark a sky! Sometimes the clouds were sulphurous yellow, sometimes black as smoke, and the dull light climbed down as on rope ladders to the ruffled sea. There were no dolphins at play or flying fishes. Once we passed a rocky reef with a lighthouse and a barrack. It was all white and shone like the mirages of palms and golden mosques on Syria's horizon.

We were not allowed ashore in Suez. Many passengers were disappointed. They had planned a quick excursion to Cairo, a camel ride to the Sphinx and the Pyramids, a visit to Tutankhamen's treasures in the museum, lunch at a luxury hotel, sightseeing at the old bazaar, dinner in the dining car—and that same evening they would have returned

---

16 'Youth', the official hymn of the Italian National Fascist Party.

to the ship in Port Said. Egypt in twelve hours, for five and a half pounds sterling!

Instead, we lay long at anchor off Suez, and I saw the desert begin in the shallow bay: from the clear beautiful blue of the gently ebbing sea the yellow sand rose and surged in long waves landwards, where no more boundary could be felt between water, sky and level ground; all glided on unhindered, elements of the same sheer light. At last we turned into the canal, with a pilot on board and engines running at half-throttle, leaving behind the city of Suez, artificially laid out on its peninsula, the white buildings and the urban promenade—and this day, though bright, though sunny, was like a moonlit night, and it was as though in some new and incomprehensible way we had left the solid ground of our world. Certainly, the canal is the work of human hands. It's about a hundred miles long, a road and a railway line run beside it, along the way there are little stations, signals, milestones. Two mighty obelisks loom on a sand dune, inclined towards each other: '1914 Défense du Canal de Suez 1918', commemorating those who died in the last World War. One feels strangely moved at the sight: humble, yet proud. But still stranger, still more incomprehensible is the sight of the desert. To glide along the still, regular, artificially blue vein of water between banks of softly sifting sand, through this unborn and barren world that is a neighbour to the cosmos, kin to unspeakable sorrow . . .

Comfort came with the cry of a gull, an Egyptian fisherman's boat gliding past. I knew, too, and tried to clearly picture it, that in the west, not far away, the Nile has watered a great valley for thousands and thousands of years. I remembered the ploughing water buffalo, the hardworking fellahs—the grace of the pharaohs' gold-painted daughters. But when evening came, and the sun slipped over edgeless horizons like a gently consuming heavenly fire, I remembered nothing more. The voyage would never end, we would never again set foot on shore, never again touch the living earth, never breathe dew and light wind in the freshness of morning!

At midnight, when our steamship reached the long harbour walls of Port Said, a little boat took us ashore through swaying garlands of festive lights. On the wharf, Simon Artz's emporium was open and awaited the foreigners. Taxi drivers, cigarette-sellers, money-changers and pimps lounged in the cross streets. The cabaret at the Oriental Exchange Hotel was already fairly deserted; the painted girls had finished their routine and drank in skimpy evening dresses with bloated elderly officers. The band played until two and did what it could. By four, the shops were closed and most of the tourists had returned to the steamship. In sadly lit pubs, sailors clung exhausted to the bars and had their whiskey glasses filled. Arab boys roamed in outlying alleys, making soft propositions in broken French and Dutch. One conjured up live chicks and made raw eggs dance on the bumpy pavement, another whispered menacingly: 'Harem ladies, pretty photos, the seven true plagues and dances of Egypt.' And behind red-lit curtains, shabby doors, musty stairwells, the painted girls sat in garish rooms, naked under their threadbare silk kimonos, and waited for the sallow light of dawn.

Adorned with white lights, the steamship slips out into the open Mediterranean. We begin the voyage home. Port Said is behind me, the night is over and done with. And I leave behind oceans, waterways, mountains, the expanses of India. I forget the desert's edge, the Khyber Pass, the cumulative mass of foreignness. I forget, forget!

In the first hour of the new day, in the cold, strong wind that already reaches our native shores, yes, in this one moment of eternally returning regret I realize: what staggers us, over and over again, is the morning splendour of departure!

'Balkan Borders' (Balkan-Grenzen)

Typescript, 14 July 1939. No evidence of publication.

'Therapia'

First published in *National-Zeitung* 154 (3 April 1940).

'Trebizond: Farewell to the Sea' (Trapezunt: Abschied vom Meer)

Typescript from June 1939. First published in *Der Bund* 509 (31 October 1939).

'Mount Ararat' (Der Ararat)

Typescript. From the collection *Die vierzig Säulen der Erinnerung* (The Forty Pillars of Memory) (Kabul, 18 December 1939). No evidence of publication.

'The Steppe' (Die Steppe)

Typescript, October 1939. First published in *National-Zeitung* 508 (1 November 1939).

'The Prisoners' (Die Gefangenen)

Typescript, July 1939. First published in *National-Zeitung* 101 (29 February 1940).

'No Man's Land: Between Persia and Afghanistan' (Niemandsland—zwischen Persien und Afghanistan)

First published in *National-Zeitung* 384 (21 August 1939).

'Herat, 1 August 1939 . . . ' (Herat, 1 August 1939 . . .)

Typescript, 1 August 1939. No evidence of publication.

'The Hindu Kush Three Times' (Dreimal der Hindukusch)
Typescript, 17 November 1939, Kabul. First published in
National-Zeitung 560 (1 December 1939).

'In the Garden of the Beautiful Girls of Qaisar' (Im Garten der
schönen Mädchen von Kaisar)
Typescript, July/August 1939. First published as 'Die Frauen
Afghanistans' (The Women of Afghanistan) in *National-
Zeitung* 172 (13/14 April 1940).

'The Women of Kabul' (Die Frauen von Kabul)
Typescript, autumn 1940. First published in *National-
Zeitung* 196 (27/28 April 1940).

'The Neighbouring Village' (Das Nachbardorf)
Typescript, November 1939. First published in *National-
Zeitung* 29 (18 January 1940).

'The Bank of the Oxus' (Das Oxus-Ufer)
Typescript, 20 November 1939. First published in *Zytglogge
Zytig* 127 (March 1988).

'The Potters of Istalif' (Die Töpfer von Istalif)
Typescript from November /December 1939. First published
in *National-Zeitung* 599 (26 December 1939).

'The Trip to Ghazni' (Die Reise nach Ghasni)
Typescript from 10 December 1939, Kabul. First published
in *Die Weltwoche* 327 (16 February 1940).

'Two Women Alone in Afghanistan' (Zwei Frauen allein in
Afghanistan)
Typescript, 13 February 1940. First published in two parts in
Thurgauer Zeitung (16/17 February 1940).

'Chehel Sotun' (Cihil Sutun)
> From *Die vierzig Säulen der Erinnerung*.

'Onward to Peshawar . . .' (Nach Peshawar . . .)
> Typescript, December 1939. First published in *Die Tat* 115 (18/19 May 1940).

'Aden, a Morning Vision' (Aden, eine Morgenvision)
> Typescript, 11 January 1940, Aden. First published in *National-Zeitung* 71 (12 February 1940).

'The Trip down the Suez Canal' (Die Reise durch den Suez-Kanal)
> Typescript, 16 January 1940, past Port Said. First published in *Luzerner Tagblatt* 233 (21 September 1940).

Afterword

'MY EXISTENCE IN THE EXILE OF
DISTANT ADVENTURE'[1]

And be it useless, / this journey. Useless and essential.
Fabio Pusterla

I

'Then [. . .], on the 31st [of December, 1938], Ella Maillart
came to visit me [. . .] I revived, finding so unexpected a
response, so direct a connection, so unmistakable a simi-
larity of mind and motive, that I was reassured and over-
joyed: I was not on the wrong path.'[2] These words mark
the beginning of one of the most unusual two-woman
endeavours in twentieth-century Swiss cultural history. At
the time she wrote them, Annemarie Schwarzenbach was
undergoing drug rehabilitation treatment in an Yverdon
clinic. She had met the Geneva-born travel writer Ella
'Kini' Maillart (1903–97) in Zurich in the early autumn of
1938. Maillart had achieved international recognition for
her adventurous trips in Asia, documented in articles and
photos. And Schwarzenbach was known in Switzerland

---

1 Annemarie Schwarzenbach, 'Diary', typescript (possibly copied
from the lost original by Ella Maillart), entry from 30 September
1939, Kabul. Photocopy with Roger Perret.

2 Letter to Alfred Wolkenberg, Yverdon, 4 January 1939. Original
with Roger Perret.

for her articles and photo essays about her travels in Europe, Asia and the US. Both were pioneers in their field and representatives of a new generation of independent, intrepid women. One could well say that, at the end of the 1930s, Schwarzenbach and Maillart were at the peak of their careers.

Released from the Yverdon clinic in late February 1939, Schwarzenbach returned to her home in Sils im Engadin. It was there that she next met with Maillart, and there that the idea of a joint trip to Afghanistan was born. Having already travelled the country by bus in 1937, Maillart wished to return, but lacked the financing and a car fit for the gruelling journey. Schwarzenbach's announcement that her father had promised her a new car—a Ford—satisfied at least one condition for the idea's realization: 'A Ford! That's the car to climb the new Hazarejat Road in Afghanistan! In Iran, too, one should travel in one's own car.'[3]

But before making concrete preparations for the journey, the pros and cons of a joint venture entailing such physical and psychological difficulty had to be carefully weighed. Would Schwarzenbach, having barely recovered from the several months of rehabilitation treatment and the draining completion of a book, survive such an exhausting journey with her health intact? Would Maillart be able to put up for long with a companion terrorized by personal and political catastrophes? Given that, unlike Schwarzenbach, she hadn't travelled with another woman

---

3 Maillart, *The Cruel Way*, p. 1.

for a long time? And hadn't her friends advised her against this trip?

Despite these misgivings, Maillart, like so many people, succumbed to the spell of Schwarzenbach's character and charisma. Once the younger woman had also expressed her admiration for the intrepid, courageous 'Kini' in a book review, the love of travel, the longing for Asia's expanses and a certain lust for discovery outweighed the differences in character and world view. Even Schwarzenbach's mother Reneé—not exactly well-disposed toward her daughter's unconventional, often risky lifestyle and plans—argued in favour of the endeavour: 'You must be able to take risks now and then—assuming you want to go on practising your profession at all. And the chance to travel with Miss Maillart isn't one you'll get often—maybe only once.'[4]

II

None of Schwarzenbach's many trips was prepared for as scrupulously and professionally as this trip to Afghanistan. The choice of cars was crucial. After various inquiries, an 18 hp Ford DeLuxe roadster was chosen and refitted in a Zurich garage for the journey's extreme demands. And Schwarzenbach, an enthusiastic driver, seems to have undergone several initiations into her new car's technical mysteries in a garage in the Engadin, as she would have to perform minor repairs herself in these remote regions.

---

4 Quoted in a letter from Annemarie Schwarzenbach to Ella Maillart, Sils-Baselgia, 12 March 1939. Photocopy with Roger Perret.

Along with the car and the projected route, the appropriate maps, driver's licences and permits had to be taken care of. Incidentally, during the trip Schwarzenbach's diplomatic passport proved indispensable for overcoming otherwise insurmountable obstacles.

Much of the space in the car was taken up by the equipment for the journalistic documenting of the trip: the two women packed typewriters, cameras, a film camera and numerous rolls of film. In order to finance the trip, they had signed a contract with the Zurich press and photographic agency Wehrle, receiving an advance of 1,000 Swiss Francs. Schwarzenbach also received advances from the publishing house Morgarten Verlag for a book on the trip and from the newspapers *Zürcher Illustrierte* and *Weltwoche*, for which she had worked previously. In May 1939, the two travelled to Paris, London and Berlin, where they visited museums, consulates, publishers, geographic societies, etc., talking with many experts to glean additional information on the best routes and the culture and politics of the countries they planned to visit.

The two had also thought long and hard about the meaning and purpose of their trip to Afghanistan. Schwarzenbach hoped it would help her get a better grip on her life—which had come close to falling apart in 1938—by giving it structure with a clearly defined goal. She also saw the strenuous journey as an opportunity to keep the temptations of morphine at bay with the help of Maillart's moral integrity. If she were to remain in Switzerland, lacking a satisfying goal in life, the cycle of depressions palliated by drugs would set in once more. For this reason she explicitly wanted the trip understood as a 'necessity'—not a 'flight'.[5]

Maillart, who travelled only 'when it is absolutely necessary for me, when I can't help it',[6] saw her own interest in the trip primarily as an ethnographic one, intending to study customs and traditions in Nuristan, a remote and culturally unique region of Afghanistan. Like her companion, she saw the endeavour as a path to self-knowledge by confronting and exploring foreign modes of thought and behaviour. Undeniably, both women were fascinated by Afghanistan because this archaic, culturally distinct and politically independent land was so remote from Europe with its climate of political insecurity. Disgust with various negative aspects of Western civilization heightened their yearning for a primordial, nomadic life in Afghanistan.

Experienced and widely travelled, Schwarzenbach and Maillart had made little fuss about their previous undertakings; this time too they were conscious that they 'did not seek adventure but merely a breathing spell, in countries where the laws of our civilization did not yet hold and where we hoped to have the singular experience that these laws are not tragic, not imperative, unalterable, indispensable.'[7] If their plan was a partial failure, it was because of

5 Letter to Maillart, Sils-Baselgia, April 1939. Photocopy with Roger Perret.

6 Cited by Schwarzenbach in 'Verbotene Reise', a review of Maillart's *Oasis interdites*, undated typescript (December 1938). Photocopy with Roger Perret.

7 Annemarie Schwarzenbach, 'Mobilisiert in Kabul' in Regina Dieterle and Roger Perret (eds), *Auf der Schattenseite* (Basel: Lenos Verlag, 1990), p. 225.

political developments as well as the specific relationship between the two women: the vulnerable, drug-addicted Schwarzenbach emerged as a manifestation of the politically and morally torn Europe that Maillart had hoped to escape.

III

On 6 June 1939, the two women drove out from Geneva. The division of labour decided before their departure functioned more or less unproblematically throughout the journey. Most of the time it was Schwarzenbach, an excellent driver, who took the wheel, 'since all that concerned the car was her domain'.[8] She was also responsible for taking most of the photographs, which would later be pooled so that Maillart could also use them to illustrate her planned travelogue.

While Schwarzenbach devoted herself to photography, Maillart operated the film camera. A comparison shows that the two women shared a common perspective, at least in this area: several of Schwarzenbach's photo motifs are strikingly similar to certain sequences in Maillart's films and seem to have been shot from the same vantage point. One recurring motif is the miracle of technology—the Ford—amid elemental landscapes, surrounded by natives marvelling as though the car came from a different planet. On the road, the car was treated almost as lovingly as a human companion, and the exploration of the vehicle's

---

8 Maillart, *The Cruel Way*, p. 13.

technical capacities seemed nearly as important as the discovery of external and internal landscapes.

By contrast, private life and reciprocal portraits play a marginal, more haphazard role. This reflects a professional attitude, the intent to use these photos and films to document foreign lands—not their own lives.

At the end of July, they crossed the border from Persia to Afghanistan. Despite minor difficulties in negotiating the northern route from Herat to Kabul—they were presumably the first women to travel it by car—by late August they reached Kabul, 'at the edge of the inhabited world'.[9] As planned, before that they had visited the Délégation Archéologique Française en Afghanistan (DAFA); the excavation leader Joseph Hackin and his wife Ria were acquaintances of Maillart.

Travelling without veils, the women caused quite a stir in this Muslim country where, except among the nomads, women were veiled and usually invisible in public. 'How does one live in the shadow of the chador?'[10] the two emancipated Europeans asked, but received no satisfactory answer. The Afghans' overwhelming hospitality made the gender issue recede into the background somewhat. Though startlingly unspoilt attitudes could be found in this country—the rejection of money as a gift of gratitude, for instance—Schwarzenbach was forced to admit: 'Neither

---

9 Letter to Arnold Kübler, Kabul, Légation de France, 21 November 1939. Estate of Arnold Kübler, Zentralbibliothek Zürich.

10 Annemarie Schwarzenbach, 'Der Tschador', *Auf der Schattenseite*, p. 234.

in Turkey, nor in Persia, nor in the Soviet Russian Caucasus did the visible, tangible incursion of a new lifestyle associated with Western technology seem to me as bitter, as devastating as in Afghanistan.'[11] Were she and Maillart conscious of using modern technology to describe and document a lifestyle that was still natural and primordial? Wasn't this technology also a product of the Western civilization whose influence in Central Asia they viewed with profound concern?

When the Second World War broke out on 3 September 1939, politics had irrevocably reached even Afghanistan, a 'state very remote from the world, and closed to it'.[12] While Schwarzenbach was able to work at the DAFA excavations on into October, Maillart had to abandon her plan to visit Nuristan. Schwarzenbach, a passionate antifascist, had been especially aware of certain harbingers of war in Europe and during their journey. Encounters with Germans who sympathized with the Nazis reinforced these dark premonitions. In Kabul, the suspicions became fact and a personal threat. 'Now it affects each one of us. And I have a foreboding of the difference between Hitler's ghastly role—and God's shadow over us.'[13] The shadow of drug addiction had followed her to the capital as well—devastated by the outbreak of war, weakened by illness and head over heels in love with Ria

11 Schwarzenbach, 'Afghanistan', typescript. Estate of Annemarie Schwarzenbach, Schweizerisches Literaturarchiv, Berne.

12 Ibid.

13 Schwarzenbach, 'Diary', Kabul, 3 September 1939.

Hackin, she was unable to withstand the poisonous temptation. For Maillart, this was a breach of the pact she had made with her friend before the journey. At the same time, she accused herself of having failed as her protector. Morally on the defensive, Schwarzenbach felt even more overwhelmed by the older woman's well-meaning advice. Later, Maillart admitted that her concerns for her psychologically unstable friend had robbed the journey of its magic.

The more politics dominated everyday life in Kabul, the clearer became the differences in the two women's political views, already evident before the trip. Influenced by Hindu and Buddhist thought, Maillart was convinced that inner enlightenment was a necessary precondition for taking on the dangerous confrontation with the chaos of the outside world: 'Why leap into a burning house—rather than stop and think where help might be found?'[14] Reacting to these words of Maillart, Annemarie asked herself: 'Seek human bliss somewhere in the Hunza Valley while my brothers, as innocent as I, die a nameless death?'[15] Her own conclusion was that the misfortunes of her fellow human beings, especially on the massive scale of war, precluded any right to personal happiness. This extreme sense of solidarity with victims and the powerless can be understood only in the light of Schwarzenbach's notion of tragedy as an essential element of existence: 'Still, time after time, pain, struggle, tension, confrontation, inner convulsion seems to me the very element of life itself.'[16]

---

14 Cited in ibid., Kabul, 30 August 1939.

15 Ibid.

16 Ibid., Kabul, 2 September 1939.

After the outbreak of war, Schwarzenbach wrote a number of articles on Central Asia's political situation in the context of events in Europe, fearing—prophetically enough—a Russian invasion of Afghanistan and referring to the country as a 'sensitive nerve centre of world politics'.[17] For all her personal hardships, she maintained her interest in political and social issues, even in 'this most foreign place'.

In Kabul, her vacillation between concern and apathy led to a certain estrangement from Maillart. With different views on how to proceed next, the two women parted in October. Schwarzenbach travelled to Turkistan, in the north of Afghanistan, where her experiences seem to have been both traumatic and cathartic. Maillart travelled to the south of India, where she led a meditative life under the guidance of the wise man Ramana Maharshi. After returning to Kabul in November, Schwarzenbach realized that 'the time for living peacefully on the sidelines [is] over. I want to return to Switzerland, not in order to hide out there, but in order to take part in what our life is.'[18] In Bombay, before boarding the ship to return to Europe in early January 1940, she met with Maillart one last time.

During the return voyage, which took nearly a month, she reflected on the journey, writing an article each day. Back home in Switzerland, she immediately began marketing the material. This proved more difficult than anticipated, as the war's all-dominating urgency dampened public interest in this rather exotic-seeming journey.

17 Schwarzenbach, 'Afghanistan'.

18 Letter to Arnold Kübler, 21 November 1939.

Nonetheless, Schwarzenbach managed to publish numerous articles, travel essays and photo reports. She gave a talk at a geographic society and also spoke on the radio about her experiences in Afghanistan.

Dissatisfied with the press agency's work while she was on the road, Schwarzenbach tried to negotiate directly with important newspapers and magazines, also helping to place Maillart's articles and photographs. The essays of the collection *The Forty Pillars of Memory*, written in Kabul, did not conform to conventional notions of travel writing and could not be used for an illustrated book about the journey; thus the publication planned with Morgarten-Verlag did not come about.

The publication of Maillart's travelogue was also long in coming. Due to Schwarzenbach's unexpected death in 1942, Maillart experienced great delays in obtaining some of her friend's documents that were crucial for the writing of the book. After the war, when she returned from India to Switzerland with the completed manuscript, Schwarzenbach's mother, Renée, asked to read the work. Only following the deletion of several passages that showed Renée's behaviour in an unfavourable light, and the use of the pseudonym 'Christina' for Maillart's deceased friend, could the book appear in England in 1947. The ambiguous title of the original edition, *The Cruel Way*, and that of the French translation, *La voie cruelle*, reflects a statement on the special nature of this joint venture which Ella Maillart made in an early stage of writing the book: 'a journey which for us was more psychological than geographical'.[19]

---

19 Letter from Ella Maillart to Anita Forrer, 17 August 1943.

The journey's true adventure was the difficult relationship between these two very different women.

IV

Travelling in order to become homeless.
Henri Michaux

Living and travelling. Travelling and writing. Writing and living. On the trip to Afghanistan it became increasingly difficult to tell one from the other.

In Afghanistan, Schwarzenbach discovered a kind of terra incognita of archaic landscapes. Sheltered from many ills of Western civilization, this land had always exercised a magical attraction for travellers. Remote from all that was familiar, the place was ideal for the self-discovery the two women desired. For 'the east was the desert, the endless waste of the sunrise, the thorny steppe of reflection'.[20] And yet, in Afghanistan, Schwarzenbach's homeland seemed strangely near: due to its mountainous landscape, its geographical situation (landlocked, surrounded by powerful neighbours), its political independence and many languages, Afghanistan is often called the 'Switzerland of Asia'. For this reason, too, the country evoked the 'childhood visions of a glorious, wide world visited by God's angels'.[21]

The concept of travel that Schwarzenbach had developed on her earlier journeys to the Middle East and

---

20 Schwarzenbach, 'Nach Westen', *Auf der Schattenseite*, p. 256.
21 Schwarzenbach, 'Afghanistan'.

Persia took on new, radical traits under the physical and psychological strain of the Afghanistan venture. She came to view travel as an especially intense form of living—'a concentrated likeness of our existence' which in contrast to today's tourism is not a 'liberation from daily routine', but 'in reality merciless'.[22] She sought to discover 'which of our habits, that protect us and blind us so, still have a genuine value'.[23] The endless succession of arrival and departure is another fundamental element of a life on the road. Though sometimes painful, however, departure can also be a 'celebration', making it possible to leave unpleasant things behind and burn overly convenient bridges. The courage to behold 'empty horizons' and chase the promise of the 'the immortal blue of the Goharshad Mosque'[24] in Herat and that of other Central Asian mosques links Schwarzenbach's motivations with those of other travellers to Asia.

And yet she asked herself, before departing for Afghanistan: 'Why do we leave this loveliest country in the world? What urges us to go east on desert roads?'[25] She supplied the answer herself: 'Surely the real motivation of

---

22 Schwarzenbach, 'The Steppe'.

23 Schwarzenbach, 'Diary', Kabul, 30 August 1939.

24 Schwarzenbach, 'No Man's Land: Between Persia and Afghanistan'.

25 Schwarzenbach, caption to the photograph 'Letzte Stunde in der Schweiz: Halt am Simplon' (The Last Hour in Switzerland— a Halt at the Simplon Pass), June 1939. Estate of Annemarie Schwarzenbach, Schweizerisches Literaturarchiv, Berne.

every true traveller is the yearning for the absolute.'[26] In Afghan Turkistan, Schwarzenbach would encounter the absolute in all its mystery. She travelled there in October 1939 with French archaeologists in order to liberate herself from the dictatorship of drugs in an inhospitable region of climatic extremes. The drastic treatment had its effect, but brought experiences of an apocalyptic nature: 'Distress and fear that cry out to Heaven, and no reply.'[27] Her sojourn and wanderings in the desert of Turkistan became a fathoming of the wasteland, the gaps in her inner landscape. Time and again, the boundaries between reality and vision seem to blur in her solitude and her radical self-confrontation.

It is no coincidence that the author alludes to Dante's *Divine Comedy* on this particular journey. She saw herself as a restless wanderer from one Hell to another, perhaps hoping through self-examination and self-flagellation to gain entrance to Purgatory and even Paradise. For this paradise, understood as a memory and an imaginary vision of 'the shore of childhood, the promised earth',[28] is the seed of the constant decampments: this 'yearning for the absolute'. And the more the absolute conceals itself in the steppes and deserts, the more powerful is its effect. In her 'Turkistan exile', Schwarzenbach equips this mythical background—the 'promised earth'—with images of Arcadian landscapes that touchingly recall those of her childhood in Bocken.

---

26 Schwarzenbach, 'Afghanistan'.

27 Schwarzenbach, 'Diary', 30 October 1939.

28 Schwarzenbach, 'Chehel Sotun'.

Thus, in the most foreign place, the dreamlike image of yearning acquires almost familiar features.

On a number of occasions, the author reports that the nearby war inside her and the distant one outside have left her speechless. At the same time, she knows that only speaking and writing can stave off the deathlike paralysis. But how could she allay her qualms about language? And how could she describe these traumatic, complicated processes? Wouldn't an account of them have to reflect an alienation that approached self-negation, the passionate searching motions which time and again missed their mark? Wouldn't the haunting, monumental landscapes and emotions have to be depicted as expressions of an all-embracing insecurity and emptiness? Wouldn't the immensity of Asia's expanses have to echo that of the white page, thus creating, as it were, an 'Asia of writing'? Couldn't aspects of the new notion of travel such as the compression and concentration of experience also be used in writing—writing as a mirror image of aimless wandering?

Even in the best pieces in this collection, such as 'Mount Ararat', 'The Steppe', 'The Hindu Kush Three Times', 'The Neighbouring Village', 'The Bank of the Oxus' and 'Chehel Sotun' (her politically and socially oriented articles do not belong to this thematic group), the author did not pursue these questions all the way. She was aware that while writing these pieces, especially the ones in *The Forty Pillars of Memory*, she was building on previous writing experiences. The pieces in this collection are particularly prone to the 'absolute sincerity' which Schwarzenbach regarded as a virtue. Thus her own ordeal is dramatically declaimed more than it is analytically illustrated. Nonetheless, these works contain unforgettable landscape descriptions that practically vibrate in the author's passionate gaze. And they confirm the fact that suffering and passion were inseparable for Schwarzenbach, that they animate and permeate her writing.

In 'The Hindu Kush Three Times', the author powerfully demonstrates the magical interplay between language and travel. Names are artfully strung like beads, in a constellation that makes it impossible to distinguish between memories of places once visited and their verbal evocation. 'What the names held'—their 'sound' and their 'colour'—reveals itself as another, mysterious reality. On the other hand, the names only develop their true power once their magic is felt 'in the flesh' and in the encounter with the things which they designate. This suggests a definition: the account of a journey is persuasive only when the language becomes a journey in its own right.

Justifiably, Annemarie Schwarzenbach wished pieces such as 'Mount Ararat' and 'Chehel Sotun' to be understood neither as articles nor as travel accounts. With their elegiac, lyrical language, they could be described as early forms of the melancholy prose poems such as 'Die zärtlichen Wege, unsere Einsamkeit' (The Tender Ways, Our Loneliness, 1940) and 'Marc' (1942) that dominated Schwarzenbach's late literary oeuvre. And as her life consisted mainly of travel, and her writing held sway over life and travel, she aptly assessed the poetic distillation of her impressions in Afghanistan as 'perhaps the only result of this journey'.

An 'incurable traveller'[29]—one who could not help 'wanting to write at all costs'.[30]

Roger Perret
Zurich, June 2000

---

29 Schwarzenbach, 'Afghanistan'.

30 Letter to Alfred Wolkenberg, 4 January 1939.